HEART-HEALTHY INSTANT POT COOKBOOK

SPINACH AND MUSHROOM SALAD, PAGE 38

HEART-HEALTHY
INSTANT POT
~ COOKBOOK ~

75 FAST AND FLAVORFUL RECIPES

LAUREN O'CONNOR

MS, RDN

ROCKRIDGE
PRESS

Interior and Cover Designer: Patricia Fabricant
Art Producer: Janice Ackerman
Editor: Justin Hartung
Production Manager: Riley Hoffman
Production Editor: Melissa Edeburn

Cover Photography: © 2022 Marija Vidal
Interior Photography: ii: ©Cameron Whitman/Stocksy; vi: ©Alicia Cho; x: ©The Picture Pantry/Stockfood; p. 18: ©Charlie Richards/StockFood; p. 34: ©Mari Moilanen/StockFood; p. 48: ©Tom J. Story; p. 66: ©Cameron Whitman/Stocksy; p. 86: ©Trent Lanz/Stocksy; p. 100: ©The Picture Pantry/Stockfood; p. 114: ©Gräfe & Unzer Verlag/Vanessa von Hilchen/StockFood; p. 128: ©Nataša Mandić/Stocksy

Paperback ISBN: 978-1-63807-757-2
eBook ISBN: 978-1-63807-762-6
R0

TO MY HUSBAND, JP, AND MY TWIN DAUGHTERS,
AILISH AND JULIA, FOR MAKING MY LIFE
JOYOUS AND COMPLETE

"BANANA BREAD" OATMEAL, PAGE 30

CONTENTS

INTRODUCTION

I have always enjoyed cooking, from the time I was six years old and making dirt-and-dandelion mud pies to recent years, where much of my work is devoted to preparing salads, main courses, and low-sugar desserts. As a culinary dietitian, my passion is to create healthy, delicious food to suit various needs and preferences.

For years, I've been interested in how even simple food combinations can elevate your taste experience while fueling your health. I became a self-proclaimed "health nut" in my early 20s, but my interest in heart health specifically grew in my 30s as I pursued a master's degree in nutritional science. I became even more focused when my stepdad was diagnosed with stage 2 hypertension. He has since passed, but I do remember the dietary, physical, and emotional changes he made to improve his condition.

For my stepdad, the transition couldn't have been easy. He was used to highly processed convenience foods, and when he cooked, he used a lot of fat and salt for flavor. He was certainly a "meat and potatoes" man—but a healthier outcome became his priority. He wasn't just lowering the sodium in his foods; treating his hypertension also required lifestyle changes, including reducing stress and preparing more heart-healthy home-cooked meals incorporating fruits and veggies, instead of relying on starch- and animal protein-heavy meals. His journey had some glitches, but he found his way toward a healthier lifestyle, and so can you.

Whether you've come to this book because you simply want to be healthier, or because you (or a loved one) had a health scare, you'll discover that "heart-healthy" and "tasty" can be synonymous. By lowering your sodium intake, trimming the saturated fat, and reaching for more whole foods, you'll likely have more energy, mental focus, and stamina, too. There is no better time than the present to pursue healthier living. Through this book, I'm happy to be your guide.

Having worked with hundreds of patients over the years, I know how hard it is for some to start (or stick to) a healthy diet. The transition is much easier when you have recipes that taste good and an appliance such as an Instant Pot that makes cooking easy. Simply fill your Instant Pot with ingredients, set it to cook, and leave the kitchen until it's done. You will enjoy the multifunctionality of the Instant Pot; you can sauté, steam, or pressure cook simply and effectively. And most important, you will appreciate how pressure cooking tenderizes meats and infuses flavor into each dish—flavor you can get using minimal oil and very little sugar and salt.

It is my hope that this book will help you embrace the benefits of a heart-healthy lifestyle as well as lead to many enjoyable meals.

BAKED APPLES WITH CRANBERRY-WALNUT FILLING, PAGE 108

CHAPTER 1
HEART-SMART FOODS IN A FLASH

The Instant Pot can help make a heart-healthy diet realistic, accessible, and absolutely delicious! In this chapter, you will discover dietary guidelines to improve your heart health, along with basic information on how to use your Instant Pot.

HEALTHY COOKING MADE SIMPLE

Healthy cooking can be a breeze, and that includes eating in a way that's beneficial to your heart. If you are looking for guidance on practical ways to follow a heart-healthy diet, you've come to the right place.

When it comes to making heart health a priority, you likely have your "why." Maybe you're recovering from heart surgery and need nourishment to properly heal. Or maybe a diagnosis of high blood pressure or high cholesterol has got you concerned. Perhaps you just want to keep up with your grandkids. Or are you tired of wheezing when you climb a flight of stairs?

If you have heart disease, it is essential to take steps to reduce your risk factors (high lipid levels, soaring cholesterol) in order to reduce clogged blood vessels and promote healthier blood flow, which allows oxygen and nutrients to be transported effectively to your organs so they can function properly. Regardless of your age or health status, heart-smart eating is a good idea. A heart-healthy diet supports your energy, mood, and ability to function—both physically and mentally.

One of the best ways to meet your heart-smart goals is to choose recipes that are balanced, delicious, and easy to prepare (even on busy weeknights). This book was designed to help you do just that. With the Instant Pot, you can prepare satisfying dishes in one versatile "set it and forget it" device while amplifying the flavors of simple, nutritious whole foods.

Before covering the essentials for using your Instant Pot, let's take a look at how eating certain foods (while limiting others) can improve your overall heart health.

BUILDING BLOCKS OF A HEART-HEALTHY DIET

There are various factors that influence a person's dietary needs, but we all can benefit from eating cardio-protective foods while minimizing excess meat, highly processed and refined foods, and alcohol. This helps reduce the saturated fat and sodium in your diet. Build your diet around some of these heart-smart foods that can help reduce your risk for heart disease.

• FRUITS AND VEGETABLES •

Fruits and veggies entice not only with their wide variety of colors and textures but with their powerful nutrient density, too. Their colors often indicate specific antioxidants; for example, the deep blue pigment of wild blueberries tells you this fruit has an intense concentration of anthocyanins, which offer antiviral and anti-inflammatory benefits. Chlorophyll, the dark green pigment that gives vegetables such as Tuscan kale their color, provides a bounty of antioxidant protection, which in turn protects your cells. Regardless of color, all fruits and vegetables contain an array of essential nutrients.

• LEAN PROTEIN •

As the building block of life, protein forms your cells, tissues, muscles—you name it! Your entire body depends on protein, which is crucial for muscle mass, strength, and healthy bones. It's also a dietary macronutrient that helps you feel satisfied. Eating protein can help boost your metabolism and lower blood pressure, too. Opt for lean proteins over foods full of saturated fat, which, when eaten in excess, can contribute to heart disease. Consuming a range of different proteins, including plant-based foods, lean animal protein, and fish, helps you meet your nutritional needs.

· VITAMINS ·

All your essential vitamins and minerals are considered heart-healthy because they work within your body in a variety of ways to promote overall health. Focus on incorporating foods that are rich in B vitamins (beans, legumes, whole grains),

THE WIDE WORLD OF HEART-HEALTHY EATING

There is no one-size-fits-all diet when it comes to health. But longstanding evidence shows that incorporating a variety of fruits and vegetables into your diet positively impacts cardiovascular health. Thus, you will find plenty of overlap in such heart-healthy diets as Mediterranean, DASH, and veganism or vegetarianism. Each of these diets is unique enough to appeal to different people for different reasons.

The MEDITERRANEAN DIET focuses on local and seasonal produce. It is a colorful diet that encourages an array of veggies, small portions of lean meats and seafood, and healthy fats.

The DASH (DIETARY APPROACHES TO STOP HYPERTENSION) DIET highlights potassium- and fiber-rich foods (fruits and vegetables) and limits saturated fat (red meats, cheese, high-fat dairy). It was designed to reduce high blood pressure.

VEGAN OR VEGETARIAN DIETS focus on whole, plant-based foods and may appeal to you if you feel strongly about the ethical treatment of animals or have specific dietary concerns. Plants are rich in dietary fiber and many nutrients important for heart health.

The main concept connecting these diets is that plant-based foods are key to healthy living. This book doesn't adhere to any one particular diet; instead, it takes a more general approach to heart-healthy eating. It's loaded with recipes that are low in saturated fat, sodium, added sugars, and cholesterol. Whether you aim to follow a Mediterranean, DASH, vegan, or vegetarian diet, you'll find plenty of recipes here to meet your needs.

calcium (broccoli, strawberries, yogurt, low-fat milk), vitamin D (mushrooms, tuna, salmon), and magnesium (nuts, seeds).

• HEALTHY FATS AND OILS •

Healthy fats include avocado, nuts and seeds, and oils such as avocado oil and olive oil. These fats are vital to your skin and hair, as well as brain and cellular function. Some include anti-inflammatory omega-3s (essential fatty acids that your body can't make on its own), while others help with nutrient absorption. For optimal health, it's important to get a diversity of these healthy fats, according to American Heart Association (AHA) guidelines.

• NUTS AND SEEDS •

These sources of healthy fat are worth calling out separately, as they provide essential nutrients such as vitamin E, zinc, copper, and selenium. They help your body absorb fat-soluble vitamins A, D, E, and K, and they also contain protein. Two tablespoons of all-natural peanut butter contains 8 grams of protein. Nuts and seeds make convenient, healthy snacks and can also provide texture and flavor to your dishes. As both nuts and seeds are calorically dense, you'll want to limit your consumption, but a handful can be plenty to help you feel satisfied.

• WHOLE GRAINS •

Whole grains provide you with energy and dietary fiber. They also contain some protein. Choose brown or wild rice, quinoa, buckwheat, oats, corn, and rye to get a variety of whole-grain goodness. Look for whole wheat bread with 3 grams of fiber or more. Foods such as pita and basmati, arborio, and jasmine rice can be included in a heart-healthy diet because they still contain some of the nutrients and carbs you need. Just remember that the more processed or refined a food is, the less germ and bran it contains, stripping it of the most nutrient-dense layer and its most fiber-rich component, respectively.

• FAT-FREE AND LOW-FAT DAIRY •

Dairy provides calcium, a nutrient essential to bone health as well as heart health, but it's important to choose fat-free or low-fat dairy products rather than those full of saturated fat. Adequate calcium levels help to maintain proper heart rhythm. Milk is fortified with vitamin D, and some cheese naturally contains it as well. Dairy also provides protein. Greek yogurt contains as much as 18 grams of protein per cup, and 1 cup of low-fat milk provides 8 grams of protein.

MAKING ADJUSTMENTS
BASED ON CONDITIONS

You may have picked up this book because you're worried about future heart problems. You may be experiencing potential symptoms of heart disease, or you may have been diagnosed with a condition that puts you at greater risk for heart disease, such as high cholesterol or diabetes. Or maybe you're recovering from cardiac surgery. Many of the nutritional recommendations for these individual situations overlap, but there are some differences to keep in mind.

• RECOVERING FROM CARDIAC SURGERY •

If you're recovering from heart surgery and have a weak appetite, you can be at risk for low energy and nutrient deficiencies. Your focus should be on eating small amounts of whole foods more often.

• HIGH CHOLESTEROL •

The main goal here is to reduce high amounts of low-density lipoprotein (LDL) cholesterol in the blood. Increase the soluble fiber in your diet by including a good amount and variety of fruits, vegetables, beans/legumes, and intact whole grains. Soluble fiber binds to LDL in your intestine, preventing it from entering your bloodstream.

• HIGH BLOOD PRESSURE •

Increasing potassium-rich foods (such as fruits and vegetables) and lowering your sodium intake are key steps to achieving the sodium-potassium balance needed to reduce hypertension (high blood pressure). Eat less meat and fewer animal products, because they are naturally higher in sodium.

• HIGH TRIGLYCERIDES •

If you have high triglycerides, you'll want to limit your total fat intake to 30 percent of your daily calories, while keeping saturated fat at or under 7 percent. You'll also want to avoid foods high in trans fats, and watch out for the simple carbs and added sugar found in highly processed convenience foods such as energy bars, crackers, chips, and cookies.

FOOD-MEDICATION INTERACTIONS

Certain foods can interact with particular medications for heart health, making them less effective or causing potential harm, so it is important to adhere to certain dietary restrictions. The following are some food-medication contraindications and recommendations. This is not a comprehensive list, so follow your doctor's advice when taking any type of medication.

STATIN DRUGS—Avoid grapefruit and other fruit juices while on these cholesterol-lowering drugs.

WARFARIN—Excess vitamin K makes this blood clot–reducing medication less effective. Limit vitamin K–rich foods, including spinach, kale, Brussels sprouts, cabbage, lettuce, chard, and green tea. Avoid grapefruit and grapefruit juice, alcohol, and cranberry juice, as they can increase your risk of bleeding while on warfarin.

ARBS, ACE INHIBITORS, SPIRONOLACTONE, HEPARIN, LABETALOL, AND PROPRANOLOL—Minimize potassium intake. Choose fruits and vegetables that are lower in potassium, and limit yourself to small portions of high-potassium produce such as avocado.

· PREDIABETES AND DIABETES ·

Aim to consume 25 to 35 grams of fiber per day. Increase your fiber intake through the consumption of whole foods such as vegetables, fruits, beans, legumes, and whole grains. Fiber, particularly soluble fiber, helps slow down the absorption of sugar to improve blood sugar levels.

BUILDING A BALANCED PLATE

Eat a variety of nutrient-dense foods so you get the balance of vitamins, minerals, and antioxidants your body needs. Every whole food—including fruits, vegetables, fish, and lean animal protein—has a unique set and amount of specific nutrients.

· MIX OF MACRONUTRIENTS ·

Your specific ratio of recommended daily macronutrients depends on your health needs. A good place to start is 15 to 20 percent protein, 55 to 60 percent carbohydrates, and 25 to 30 percent fat. As you see, there is some wiggle room here, and you should consult with a registered dietitian for specific recommendations.

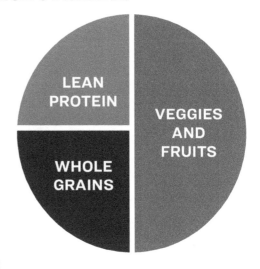

A general guideline to remember: Fill half your plate with veggies and fruits, a quarter with lean protein, and a quarter with whole grains. Get in a little healthy fat (which includes the oil you use while cooking), too; a few nuts or small slices of avocado are a nice way to garnish your meal while supplying your body with heart-healthy fats.

· PORTION CONTROL ·

Keep an eye on your portion sizes to achieve healthy weight goals. Try to keep lean beef or fish to 4 to 6 ounces per serving, cooked veggies to ½ cup (or raw veggies to 1 cup), and whole grains, beans, or legumes to ½ cup.

Using smaller plates can make it easier to stick to smaller portions—try eating on 6-inch plates versus standard 10- to 12-inch dinner plates. Measuring cups can be helpful as well. And even a standard ice cream scoop can help you portion out perfect rounded ½-cup portions.

· DAILY CALORIC INTAKE ·

Depending on your size and stature, activity level, and health condition, caloric intakes vary considerably. For an average-size person who is relatively active, a diet of 2,000 calories per day may be recommended for weight maintenance; most labels include dietary values (DV) based on a 2,000-calorie diet. However, specific needs can range from 1,200 to 1,600 calories per day to as many as 3,000 or more. Consult with a dietitian to find out your specific needs and adjust your plating as necessary.

FOODS TO LOVE, LIMIT, OR LET GO

This table looks at different categories of foods to enjoy, limit, or let go. The "To Love" category is not an encouragement of endless consumption, but rather indicates that the food is a better choice for your heart when eaten as part of a well-balanced meal. Still limit grains to ½ cup per serving and lean meat, fish, and poultry to 4 to 6 ounces per serving, depending on your individual needs.

FOODS	TO LOVE
GRAINS	Whole grains (oats, quinoa, farro, bulgur, buckwheat, whole wheat couscous, whole wheat pasta, whole barley, and brown rice)
DAIRY	Organic nonfat/low-fat yogurt, and kefir
FISH	Wild salmon, arctic char, sardines, branzino, halibut, rainbow trout, Pacific cod, Atlantic sea bass, and barramundi
POULTRY AND MEATS	Skinless chicken breast, skinless turkey breast, and lean ground chicken or turkey
SOY	Organic tofu, tempeh, edamame, cooked soybeans, and soy milk
LEGUMES	Sprouted and boiled beans, BPA-free canned beans (no-salt-added or low-sodium, or rinsed), and Tetra Pak low-sodium beans
NUTS AND SEEDS	Raw and unsalted nuts and seeds (such as walnuts, almonds, pistachios, chia seeds, flaxseed, and pumpkin seeds) and nut butters (with only the nut as the first ingredient)
VEGETABLES	Vegetables (no added salt)
FRUITS	Fruit (no added sugar)
OILS	Olive oil, avocado oil, and sesame oil
BEVERAGES	Water and teas (green, black, oolong, and hibiscus)

TO LIMIT	TO LET GO
Whole wheat bread, whole-grain sourdough, and basmati and arborio rice	Refined carbohydrates (such as high-sugar cereals and white breads)
Low-fat cow's milk, part-skim mozzarella cheese, cottage cheese, ricotta cheese, and feta cheese	Processed cheese (such as Velveeta), most full-fat dairy, and yogurt with added sugar
Mackerel, tuna, red snapper, shellfish, and tilapia	Flounder, swordfish, tilefish, herring, and anchovies
Skinless chicken thighs, skinless chicken drumsticks, lean beef, grass-fed meat, and pork loin	Fried chicken, deli and processed meats (such as bacon and sausage), and fatty cuts of meat (such as heavily marbled meats, rib eye steak, strip steak, skirt steak, pork butt or round, pork belly)
Miso paste, low-sodium soy sauce, and low-sodium tamari	Processed soy (such as textured soy protein, soy protein isolate, and soybean oil)
Canned beans with more than 250mg sodium per serving (rinsing and draining may reduce sodium by up to 41%)	Sodium-rich canned beans (600mg or more sodium per serving), refried beans, and baked beans
Prepackaged roasted, salted seeds and nuts (limit to 1 ounce or about ¼ cup serving).	Processed nut butters with hydrogenated oils or palm oil
Canned vegetables with more than 250mg sodium per serving.	Creamed or sodium-rich (600mg or more sodium per serving) canned or frozen vegetables, French fries, and fried (including batter-fried) vegetables
No-sugar-added dried fruit and unsweetened coconut flakes	Sugar-added dried fruit, jams, and juices
	Vegetable shortening, hydrogenated oils, palm oil, coconut oil, margarine, ghee, and butter
Coffee and red wine	Soda, diet soda, energy drinks, and fruit juices

INSTANT POT 101

At its core, the Instant Pot is a smart, programmable multicooker, meaning it includes a multitude of cooking modes and methods. It can sauté, pressure cook, slow cook, steam, and sterilize—all in the same vessel. It also acts as a warmer. You can use your Instant Pot to make yogurt, rice, soup, stews—the list goes on and on.

Unlike the pressure cookers of yore, the Instant Pot doesn't require careful attention. While it works its cooking magic, you can hang out in the kitchen or binge watch your favorite show. The timer lets you know when cooking has finished. Even then, it automatically moves into Keep Warm mode, so you don't have to attend to it as soon as the timer goes off.

Most people turn to the Instant Pot because of its pressure-cooking capabilities. The term "pressure cooking" simply refers to the process of using liquid in a sealed vessel to cook food. When heated, the liquid begins to boil. The sealed pot traps in the steam from the boiling process. This causes the pressure and temperature in the pot to rise at a very fast rate, cooking the ingredients quickly.

· INSTANT POT BENEFITS ·

The Instant Pot uses the same pressure-cooking engineering and mechanics as stovetop models, but it provides some additional—and significant—advantages.

Speed—Compared to traditional stovetop cooking, the Instant Pot can cut cooking times by as much as 75 percent. For example, dried beans cooked in a pot on the stovetop can take from 40 minutes to 3 hours. The Instant Pot cuts those cooking times by one-third to one-half, depending on the type of bean and whether you presoaked them.

Ease and convenience—With the simple press of a button, the machine can preheat itself and automatically switch to the setting you've selected. Once finished, it then automatically switches to the Keep Warm setting. Another convenience is the quick pressure release, which allows for fine control over cooking time, creating perfectly finished meals.

More flavor and less fat—Because the Instant Pot locks in flavors and moisture by keeping the contents sealed under pressure, you won't need as much butter or oil in your recipes. For recipes that use the Sauté function, you'll need less oil to prevent sticking if you heat the inner pot first (30 seconds), then add the oil and let it heat for 30 seconds, and finally, add the food.

No-oil cooking options—Poaching is one of the simplest ways to prepare an egg, chicken breast, or salmon without using oil. You can also easily prepare sous vide eggs in your Instant Pot.

Nutrition—Instant Pot cooking methods retain up to 90 percent of the vitamins and minerals in foods, compared to stovetop cooking. Additionally, it allows you to steam, poach, sous vide, and prepare flavorful veggie-rich soups and stews with ease, making it an essential tool for heart-healthy cooking.

Cleaning—It is easy to clean and maintain an Instant Pot. That said, sometimes you'll need to put some extra effort into removing set-in foods to prevent them from flavoring your next meal.

HOW TO USE YOUR INSTANT POT

Whether you're preparing a weeknight dinner for two or a weekend dinner party for 12, most Instant Pot recipes call for the same cooking steps. The good news is, they aren't complicated and usually require only the push of a button.

Precooking ingredients—Not all recipes call for precooking, but if one does, it usually involves sautéing. For example, Blistered Snap Peas with Yogurt Cheese (page 39) requires that you first sauté the snap peas to get a crisp, browned crust before combining them with the other ingredients.

Adding liquid—Most recipes call for a liquid such as water or broth. It's also important to add a sufficient amount of liquid for the size of your Instant Pot. When steaming vegetables in a steaming basket, first pour the water into the Instant Pot, then place the trivet in the pot and the steamer basket with the vegetables on top of that (vegetables cooked in larger pieces can be placed directly on the trivet). For beans, add them first and then pour in the water.

Locking the lid into place—It's crucial that before you begin pressure cooking, the steam-release knob is in the Sealing position (versus Venting). If it's not, the pot won't build pressure.

Selecting the setting, adjusting pressure, and indicating the cooking time—To pressure cook, set the pressure level (High or Low), then enter the cook time. (Note: Not every model has a Start button. Some displays will change to ON after you set the cook time. The cooking begins 10 seconds after that. Initially, you may hear a soft sound; this is the machine building pressure. If the sound is loud, make sure the lid is locked properly.) If you're using a preset function, press the appropriate button when you're ready to cook.

Releasing pressure—After cooking, pressure can be manually released quickly or allowed to dissipate naturally. Release the pressure according to the recipe's instructions. To quick release, press Cancel and move the steam-release knob to the Venting position. (Some models also have a steam-release button that needs to be pressed after moving the knob.) To release the pressure naturally, press Cancel and wait for the pressure to come down on its own—usually 15 to 20 minutes. Some recipes call for a natural release for a specific time and then a quick release of any remaining pressure. If that's the case, let the pressure release naturally for the indicated time, then move the steam-release knob to the Venting position to quick release the remaining pressure.

INSTANT POT TROUBLESHOOTING

Here are solutions to some of the most common Instant Pot problems.

Pressure cooking hasn't started after 20 minutes.

Check the condition of the sealing ring. If it's damaged, that could be a reason the pot won't cook.

I got a "Burn" warning.

This warning is a new feature of more recent models. It is triggered when there isn't enough liquid in the pot to allow pressure to build. If you get a "Burn" warning, add more liquid to the pot and stir, scraping up any browned bits from the bottom, then restart the cooking cycle. If the ingredients are fully scorched, empty the pot, clean it, and start over.

My pudding smells like curry.

The sealing ring absorbs the flavors of anything you cook, so it's important to clean the ring after each use. Even better: Have separate rings for savory recipes and sweet recipes.

My steam-release knob is clogged.

If you use too much liquid, your recipe will become frothy, which can clog the steam-release knob. If the knob is clogged, remove the anti-block shield, carefully clean it, and place it back in the Instant Pot.

My food is always dry or overcooked.

After cooking, the Instant Pot moves to Keep Warm mode, which can cause foods to dry out or overcook. Instead, you can just unplug the Instant Pot, then, when you're ready to serve, press Keep Warm to reheat.

The float valve isn't rising.

Food particles sometimes get released during the cooking process and collect on the float valve, which prevents it from rising. If stuck, remove it from the lid, thoroughly clean it, and reattach. Check to see if the silicone cap is damaged, and replace it if necessary.

I can't open or close the lid.

This occurs if the sealing ring isn't property set. Simply unlock and remove the lid after the float valve drops. Move the steam-release knob to Venting, and when the pressure completely drops, open the lid.

STOCKING YOUR
HEART-HEALTHY KITCHEN

Before you start delving into the recipes, be sure your kitchen is stocked wisely. That means having heart-smart pantry staples such as herbs and spices (and blends like Italian seasoning or za'atar), condiments like low-sodium Worcestershire and soy sauce, and healthy oils such as olive oil and avocado oil.

· FRIDGE STAPLES ·

Fresh ingredients are the backbone of many of the recipes in this book. Some items to stock up on include:

- Leafy greens (spinach, arugula)
- Eggs
- Low-fat (1%) milk or unsweetened plant milks, including soy milk and almond milk
- Tofu
- Wild-caught salmon
- Low-fat plain Greek yogurt
- Low-fat (2%) cottage cheese
- Low-fat or part-skim ricotta cheese

· PANTRY STAPLES ·

The versatility of the following items will keep your pantry load relatively small:

- Spices and herbs: garlic powder, black pepper, cinnamon, Italian seasoning, za'atar
- Condiments, sauces, and flavorings: low-sodium soy sauce, low-sodium Worcestershire sauce, vanilla extract, Dijon mustard, low-sodium ketchup, low-sodium marinara sauce
- Beans: low-sodium canned or dried lentils, chickpeas, black beans, kidney beans
- Whole grains: brown rice, kasha, oats, quinoa
- Nuts and seeds: almonds, walnuts, pistachios

HEART-SMART SHOPPING TIPS

There are a few things to remember while grocery shopping to help you make heart-smart choices and keep your fridge stocked with healthy foods:

1. **Read food labels.** Many canned products, convenience items, and frozen entrées contain sodium levels (and saturated fat) well above the recommended limits per serving. Take a moment to scan the label to ensure a single serving contains less than 600 milligrams of sodium and that the saturated fat is no more than 3.5 grams per serving. Always check the serving size, too!

2. **Shop the produce aisle first.** In many grocery stores, produce is housed along the periphery of the market. Load your cart with a variety of fruits and veggies to start, then gather your whole grains and legumes. Focus more on whole-plant foods and less on meat and dairy.

3. **Choose low-sodium options.** Whenever possible, buy low-sodium or no-salt-added beans, marinara sauce, and condiments such as soy sauce and Worcestershire sauce. These healthier options still provide plenty of flavor!

4. **Watch out for added sugars.** Skip processed snacks such as energy bars and treats. Again, always scan the label—even healthier-sounding items can be high in added sugars. Pass on any product that contains more than 8 grams of added sugar per serving.

5. **Avoid shopping on an empty stomach.** When you're hungry, it's harder to make heart-smart choices and you'll be much more likely to fill your cart with items you don't need. Make sure you eat something before you head to the store, and stick to your grocery list once you're there.

· EQUIPMENT ESSENTIALS ·

While recipes in this book don't require a lot of gadgets or tools beyond the Instant Pot and the accessories that come with it (such as the wire trivet), be sure to have some common cookware such as a set of measuring cups, a wire whisk, a set of mixing bowls, spatulas, and sharp knives for cutting (you'll need a paring knife for stone fruits and a medium/large chef's knife for meats and produce), a set of tongs, and a colander. Beyond those, you'll want to have:

- A stand mixer or handheld mixer for fluffy egg whites
- An immersion blender or standing blender for pureeing
- A few 6-inch round cake pans, including at least one springform pan for easy release
- A 7-cup silicone egg mold (or a set of silicone muffin liners) for poached and sous-vide eggs, as well as biscuits and brownies
- A set of mini or standard ramekins or 4-ounce canning jars
- A 6-inch metal steamer basket

6 WAYS TO MAKE A HEART-HEALTHY DIET EASIER

In addition to cooking the heart-healthy recipes in this book, there are some other things you can include in your lifestyle to make healthy eating a long-lasting venture.

1 **Refresh your pantry.** Clear your pantry of highly processed foods such as pretzels, chips, and bars. Make more space for whole-food items like legumes, intact whole grains (rice, quinoa, buckwheat, oats), versatile spices and herbs, and low-sodium condiments. This will help reduce sodium and saturated fat.

2 **Batch cook and prep ahead.** Creating meals ahead of time saves you countless hours in the kitchen, so make that large pot of stew and you'll have meals ready to reheat and serve.

3 **Create a flexible meal plan.** Choose three dinners you'd like to make for the week. This will help inform your shopping list, so you can buy just what you need (and won't need to make repeat trips to the market). Make sure to choose recipes that provide easy, tasty leftovers.

4 **Pack your lunches.** Prepare your midday meal in advance. That way, when hunger strikes, you'll be less likely to order takeout or nibble out of your fridge.

5 **Make meal prepping a group activity.** Enlist family or friends to help with prepping. They'll have fun and enjoy the great meal they've helped with.

6 **Schedule themes for particular days of the week.** Plan some fun, healthy nights like Taco Tuesdays or Fish Fridays to keep mealtimes fun and creative.

THIS BOOK'S RECIPES

The recipes in this book have been designed with your heart health in mind. The amount of sodium, saturated fat, and added sugar in each meal or dish was carefully considered. Plenty of plant foods keep recipes antioxidant-rich and full of dietary fiber.

Complete meals in this book include protein, complex carbs, and vegetables and have 500 or fewer calories, no more than 600 milligrams of sodium, 3.5 grams or less of saturated fat, and no more than 8 grams of added sugar per serving. Individual dishes (such as breakfasts without sides) contain fewer calories and have a lower limit on sodium (360 milligrams or less), and appetizers and snacks have no more than 250 calories with a sodium limit of 240 milligrams per serving.

The recipes include dietary labels—Vegan, Vegetarian, Dairy-Free, and Gluten-Free—to help you quickly find recipes that are right for your particular way of eating. Some recipes also include convenience labels: 5 or Fewer Ingredients (excluding water and pantry staples, cooking spray, oil, salt, and pepper), One-Pot (no need for anything other than your Instant Pot!), Quick (30 minutes or less from start to finish), and Worth the Wait (more than 45 minutes, but worth it!). Finally, you'll find tips for recipe variations and ingredient substitutions, advice for prepping specific ingredients, and ways to add a flavor boost.

Note: The Total Time in each recipe includes a 6- to 8-minute pressure build (and time to prepare a sauce or staple recipe from chapter 8, if using one).

EGGS BENEDICT WITH LOW-FAT BÉCHAMEL SAUCE, **PAGE 24**

CHAPTER 2
BREAKFAST AND BRUNCH

SOUS-VIDE EGG BITES WITH FENNEL AND MUSHROOMS

GLUTEN-FREE | VEGETARIAN

These flavorful egg bites have 122 milligrams of calcium per serving, meeting nearly 10 percent of your recommended daily value. And with mushrooms in the mix, you've got a natural source of vitamin D.

Makes 7 egg bites
Prep time: 5 minutes
Cook time: 12 minutes at high pressure
Pressure release: Natural for 10 minutes, then Quick
Total time: 32 minutes

Nonstick cooking spray

1½ cups water

4 medium eggs

1 cup low-fat cottage cheese

½ cup chopped mushrooms

2 tablespoons grated fennel bulb

2 garlic cloves, minced

¼ cup grated Parmesan cheese

PER SERVING (2 EGG BITES): Calories 132, Total Fat 7g, Saturated Fat 3g, Cholesterol 172mg, Sodium 263mg, Potassium 144mg, Magnesium 8mg, Carbohydrates 4g, Sugars 2g, Added Sugars 0g, Fiber 0.2g, Protein 12g, Vitamin K 2mcg

1 Coat a 7-cup silicone egg mold with nonstick spray. Pour 1½ cups of water into the Instant Pot and set the trivet in the center. Place the egg mold on top.

2 In a medium bowl, whisk the eggs until fluffy. Stir in the cottage cheese, mushrooms, fennel, garlic, and Parmesan until well combined.

3 Fill each well of the egg mold with ¾ cup of the egg mixture. Cover the mold with its lid or aluminum foil.

4 Lock the lid into place. Select Pressure Cook and cook on high pressure for 12 minutes. When the cooking is complete, allow the pressure to release naturally for 10 minutes, then quick release any remaining pressure and remove the lid.

5 Remove the egg mold and let the egg bites rest at room temperature for 2 minutes before serving.

Variation Tip: Toss ½ cup of frozen chopped veggies into the egg mixture to add some color and a bit of texture to this dish.

SOFT-BOILED EGG BITES WITH APRICOT CHEESE TOASTS

VEGETARIAN | QUICK

Soft-boiled eggs are comforting and nutritious! Egg yolks provide the heart-healthy B vitamins B$_{12}$ and folate, as well as fat-soluble vitamins A, D, E, and K and some omega-3s.

Serves 4
Prep time: 5 minutes
Cook time: 3 minutes at high pressure
Pressure release: Quick
Total time: 13 minutes

4 slices whole-grain bread, toasted

½ cup low-fat ricotta

¼ cup plus 2 tablespoons water

7 or 8 medium apricots, pitted and sliced

1 tablespoon honey

1 cinnamon stick

Nonstick cooking spray

4 medium eggs

PER SERVING: Calories 215, Total Fat 8g, Saturated Fat 3g, Cholesterol 177mg, Sodium 277mg, Potassium 375mg, Magnesium 35mg, Carbohydrates 24g, Sugars 11g, Added Sugars 2.2g, Fiber 3g, Protein 14g, Vitamin K 5mcg

1 Divide the toast among four plates and spread 2 tablespoons of ricotta on each. Set aside.

2 Combine the water, apricots, honey, and cinnamon stick in the Instant Pot. Place an upside-down ramekin in the center and set the trivet on top, so that it's raised at least 1 inch above the fruit mixture.

3 Coat a 7-cup silicone egg mold with nonstick spray. Crack each egg into a well in the mold and carefully place the mold on the trivet.

4 Lock the lid into place. Select Pressure Cook and cook on high pressure for 3 minutes. When the cooking is complete, quick release the pressure. Remove the lid and lift out the egg mold, trivet, and ramekin. The egg yolks should be soft and sticky; nearly set, but not firm. Discard the cinnamon stick from the apricot mixture.

5 Use a spoon to transfer one egg bite to each ricotta-topped toast, then scoop ¼ cup of the apricot mixture over each piece of toast and serve.

Ingredient Tip: The longer you steam your egg, the harder the yolk will be. If you prefer a softer, runny yolk, cook on high pressure for only 2 minutes.

BREAKFAST BURRITO

VEGETARIAN

Although breakfast burritos may seem quite fattening, you can enjoy them while sticking to your heart-smart goals by making this easy Instant Pot version. Garlic, cumin, and coriander add flavor in place of salt, while red and green bell peppers add color plus vitamin C to help control blood pressure. When buying tortillas, look for ones with at least 40 percent less sodium.

Serves 4
Prep time: 5 minutes
Sauté: 3 minutes
Cook time: 15 minutes at high pressure
Pressure release: Natural for 10 minutes, then Quick
Total time: 38 minutes

2 teaspoons olive oil
¼ teaspoon ground cumin
¼ teaspoon ground coriander
½ teaspoon garlic powder
4 ounces extra-firm tofu, diced
½ teaspoon low-sodium soy sauce
1½ cups water
Nonstick cooking spray
3 medium eggs
¼ cup plus 2 tablespoons plain low-fat Greek yogurt
1 small red bell pepper, thinly sliced
1 small green bell pepper, thinly sliced
4 reduced-sodium flour tortillas
2 loose cups baby arugula

1. Select Sauté and wait 30 seconds for the Instant Pot to warm. Pour in the oil and heat for 30 seconds, until it sizzles. Stir in the cumin, coriander, and garlic powder and cook for 30 seconds, until the aromas release. Add the tofu and cook for 1 minute. Transfer the tofu mixture to a bowl and stir in the soy sauce. Set aside.

2. Pour 1½ cups of water into the Instant Pot and set the trivet in the center. Coat a 6-inch round cake pan with nonstick spray.

3. In a medium bowl, whisk together the eggs, ¼ cup of yogurt, and the bell peppers. Pour the egg mixture into the prepared cake pan and cover with aluminum foil, then place the cake pan on the trivet.

4. Lock the lid into place. Select Pressure Cook and cook on high pressure for 15 minutes.

5. While the eggs are cooking, spread an even layer of the remaining 2 tablespoons yogurt onto each tortilla.

6. When the cooking is complete, allow the pressure to release naturally for 10 minutes, then quick release any remaining pressure and remove the lid.

PER SERVING: Calories 252, Total Fat 10g, Saturated Fat 3g, Cholesterol 125mg, Sodium 285mg, Potassium 254mg, Magnesium 17mg, Carbohydrates 26g, Sugars 3g, Added Sugars 0g, Fiber 2g, Protein 13g, Vitamin K 18mcg

7   Stir the egg mixture with a fork to give it a "scrambled egg" texture. Divide the egg mixture and tofu evenly over the tortillas, then top evenly with the arugula. Working with one at a time, fold in the sides of the tortillas and roll up to enclose the filling.

8   Divide the burritos among four plates and serve.

Variation Tip: You can swap out the bell pepper for ¾ cup of chopped tomato. Add the tomato to the egg mixture prior to cooking, or serve it raw as a burrito filling, adding it along with the arugula.

EGGS BENEDICT WITH LOW-FAT BÉCHAMEL SAUCE

VEGETARIAN | QUICK

Served on an English muffin with spinach and a drizzle of low-fat béchamel, this lightened eggs Benedict is yummy, even without the bacon.

Serves 4
Prep time: 7 minutes
Cook time: 2 minutes at high pressure
Pressure release: Quick
Total time: 14 minutes

1½ cups water

Nonstick cooking spray

4 medium eggs

¾ cup low-fat milk

1 medium egg yolk

1 tablespoon all-purpose flour

¼ teaspoon garlic powder

1 tablespoon grated Parmesan cheese

Juice of 1 lemon

Freshly ground black pepper (optional)

2 whole wheat English muffins, split and toasted

2 cups baby spinach

PER SERVING: Calories 187, Total Fat 7g, Saturated Fat 2.4g, Cholesterol 207mg, Sodium 237mg, Potassium 303mg, Magnesium 47mg, Carbohydrates 20g, Sugars 6g, Added Sugars 1g, Fiber 3g, Protein 12g, Vitamin K 73mcg

1 Pour 1½ cups of water into the Instant Pot and set the trivet in the center.

2 Coat a 7-cup silicone egg mold with nonstick spray. Crack each egg into a well of the egg mold. Cover the mold with its lid or aluminum foil and set it on the trivet.

3 Lock the lid into place. Select Pressure Cook and cook on high pressure for 2 minutes. When the cooking is complete, quick release the pressure. Remove the lid and lift out the egg mold and the trivet. Dump out the water, dry the inner pot, and return it to the Instant Pot.

4 Pour the milk and egg yolk into the inner pot. Select Sauté and cook, whisking continuously, for 30 seconds, until thoroughly combined. Whisk in the flour, garlic powder, and Parmesan; keep whisking until the liquid comes to a boil and starts to thicken. Press Cancel and stir in the lemon juice. Season with black pepper (if using).

5 Divide the English muffin halves among four plates. Top each muffin half with ½ cup of spinach, 1 poached egg, and ¼ cup of béchamel sauce and serve.

LEMON RICOTTA PANCAKE BITES

VEGETARIAN | QUICK

These pancake bites come out softer and fluffier than a traditional griddle cake, but the overall result is tasty and satisfying. The blueberries add sweetness to complement the pancakes' flavor and anti-inflammatory benefits, too!

Serves 4
Prep time: 10 minutes
Cook time: 7 minutes at high pressure
Pressure release: Natural for 7 minutes, then Quick
Total time: 29 minutes

2 medium eggs, separated

¾ cup low-fat milk

1 teaspoon olive oil or avocado oil

1 cup all-purpose flour

1 teaspoon baking powder

1½ cups water

Nonstick cooking spray

¾ cup low-fat ricotta cheese, divided

Juice of 1 lemon

2 tablespoons maple syrup

2 cups thawed frozen wild blueberries

PER SERVING: Calories 193, Total Fat 4g, Saturated Fat 1.4g, Cholesterol 51mg, Sodium 194mg, Potassium 248mg, Magnesium 15mg, Carbohydrates 33g, Sugars 17g, Added Sugars 6g, Fiber 2g, Protein 8g, Vitamin K 12mcg

1 In a medium bowl, whip the egg whites with a hand mixer until soft peaks form.

2 In a separate medium bowl, whisk together the egg yolks, milk, and oil. Stir in the flour and baking powder until well combined. Gently fold in the whipped egg whites.

3 Pour 1½ cups of water into the Instant Pot and set the trivet in the center.

4 Coat a 7-cup silicone egg mold with nonstick spray. Pour the batter into the egg mold, filling each well about halfway. Add a small dollop (about 1 rounded teaspoon) of ricotta into the center of the batter in each well; reserve the remaining ricotta for serving. Cover the mold with its lid or aluminum foil and place it on the trivet.

5 Lock the lid into place. Select Pressure Cook and cook on high pressure for 7 minutes. When the cooking is complete, allow the pressure to release naturally for 7 minutes, then quick release any remaining pressure and remove the lid. Remove the egg mold.

6 In a small bowl, combine the lemon juice and maple syrup.

7 Serve 2 pancake bites with 1 tablespoon of maple-lemon syrup, 2 tablespoons of the reserved ricotta, and ½ cup of blueberries.

FRENCH TOAST SOUFFLÉ

VEGETARIAN

Why soak your French toast overnight when you can pressure-cook it to perfection? Making this recipe in the Instant Pot seals in the moistness and flavor. Whipped egg whites give this dish a soufflé texture. Whole-grain bread with at least 3 grams of fiber per slice provides a dose of dietary roughage and B vitamins.

Serves 4
Prep time: 5 minutes
Cook time: 15 minutes at high pressure
Pressure release: Natural for 10 minutes, then Quick
Total time: 35 minutes

1½ cups water

Nonstick cooking spray

3 medium eggs, separated

½ cup low-fat cottage cheese

1 tablespoon honey

½ teaspoon vanilla extract

2 slices whole wheat bread, toasted and quartered

½ cup canned unsweetened sliced peaches, drained

1 cup plain low-fat Greek yogurt

½ teaspoon ground cinnamon

1. Pour 1½ cups of water into the Instant Pot and set the trivet in the center. Coat a 6-inch round cake pan with nonstick spray.

2. In a medium bowl, whip the egg whites with a hand mixer until soft peaks form.

3. In a separate medium bowl, mix together the egg yolks, cottage cheese, honey, and vanilla. Gently fold in the egg whites until well combined. Submerge the pieces of toast in the mixture and gently stir in the peaches.

4. Pour the batter into the prepared cake pan and cover with aluminum foil, then place the pan on the trivet.

5. Lock the lid into place. Select Pressure Cook and cook on high pressure for 15 minutes. When the cooking is complete, allow the pressure to release naturally for 10 minutes, then quick release any remaining pressure and remove the lid.

PER SERVING: Calories 235, Total Fat 7g, Saturated Fat 2.4g, Cholesterol 131mg, Sodium 314mg, Potassium 286mg, Magnesium 43mg, Carbohydrates 26g, Sugars 11g, Added Sugars 6g, Fiber 3g, Protein 18g, Vitamin K 4mcg

6   Remove the cake pan. Slice the soufflé into 4 wedges and use a small spatula to gently remove each slice.

7   Serve each wedge with 2 tablespoons of yogurt and a dusting of cinnamon.

Variation Tip: To sweeten this dish, reserve 1 tablespoon of the juices from the canned peaches and stir it into the yogurt before dolloping onto each souffle (this will add 2 grams of added sugar).

BISCUITS AND BERRIES

VEGETARIAN

A warm, fluffy biscuit can turn a boring Sunday breakfast into a brunch-worthy treat. And who says biscuits don't fit into a heart-healthy plan? Compared to regular biscuits, this vegetarian option has less saturated fat and requires only minimal oil. Whipped egg whites give these biscuits a light and springy texture.

Serves 4
Prep time: 5 minutes
Cook time: 7 minutes at high pressure
Pressure release: Natural for 5 minutes, then Quick
Total time: 35 minutes (including cooling time)

FOR THE BERRY COMPOTE

1½ cups water
8 ounces frozen mixed berries
2 teaspoons cornstarch
2 teaspoons brown sugar

FOR THE BISCUITS

Nonstick cooking spray
2 medium eggs, separated
¼ cup low-fat milk
1 cup all-purpose flour
1 teaspoon baking powder
⅛ teaspoon salt
1 tablespoon avocado oil

TO MAKE THE BERRY COMPOTE

1 Pour 1½ cups of water into the Instant Pot and set the trivet in the center.

2 In a 6-inch round cake pan, combine the berries, cornstarch, and brown sugar. Cover with aluminum foil. Set the cake pan on the trivet.

TO MAKE THE BISCUITS

3 Coat a 7-cup silicone egg mold with non-stick spray.

4 In a medium bowl, whip the egg whites with a hand mixer until soft peaks form.

5 In a separate medium bowl, whisk together the egg yolks and milk until well combined.

6 In a third medium bowl, combine the flour, baking powder, and salt. Mix in the oil with a fork, then mix in the egg yolk mixture. Gently fold in the egg whites until well incorporated.

PER SERVING: Calories 307, Total Fat 8g, Saturated Fat 2g, Cholesterol 110mg, Sodium 317mg, Potassium 117mg, Magnesium 15mg, Carbohydrates 49g, Sugars 11g, Added Sugars 3g, Fiber 3g, Protein 9g, Vitamin K 3mcg

7   Pour the mixture into the wells of the egg mold, filling each three-quarters full. Cover the mold with its lid or aluminum foil, then place the egg mold on top of the cake pan in the Instant Pot.

8   Lock the lid into place. Select Pressure Cook and cook on high pressure for 7 minutes. When the cooking is complete, allow the pressure to release naturally for 5 minutes, then quick release any remaining pressure and remove the lid.

9   Transfer the egg mold to a wire rack. Remove the cake pan from the pot and remove the foil. Let the berries cool for 10 to 15 minutes, until the mixture has thickened.

10 Divide the biscuits evenly among four plates, top with the berry compote, and serve.

"BANANA BREAD" OATMEAL

GLUTEN-FREE | ONE-POT | VEGETARIAN | QUICK

Not only is this banana bread–inspired oatmeal heart-protective—it's good for digestion, too! Bananas are easy on the stomach and a good source of potassium (which is good for blood pressure regulation). Walnuts deliver anti-inflammatory omega-3s. And don't forget the value of oats, supplying both soluble and insoluble fiber—the former helps manage cholesterol, while the latter keeps you regular.

Serves 4
Prep time: 5 minutes
Cook time: 3 minutes at high pressure
Pressure release: Quick
Total time: 13 minutes

1 cup low-fat milk or unsweetened almond milk

1 cup water

1½ cups gluten-free rolled oats

2 medium bananas, sliced, divided

4 small dates, pitted and thinly sliced

½ teaspoon vanilla extract

½ cup chopped walnuts

1 cup blueberries (optional)

PER SERVING (⅔ CUP): Calories 284, Total Fat 12g, Saturated Fat 2g, Cholesterol 3mg, Sodium 32mg, Potassium 419mg, Magnesium 83mg, Carbohydrates 38g, Sugars 12g, Added Sugars 0g, Fiber 5g, Protein 9g, Vitamin K 1.4mcg

1 In the Instant Pot, combine the milk, water, oats, 1 sliced banana, the dates, and vanilla.

2 Lock the lid into place. Select Pressure Cook and cook on high pressure for 3 minutes. When the cooking is complete, quick release the pressure and remove the lid.

3 Spoon the oatmeal into bowls and top each evenly with the walnuts, the remaining banana slices, and blueberries, if desired, then serve.

Ingredient Tip: For heartier texture and nuttier flavor, you can swap rolled oats for an equal portion of steel-cut oats (McCann's Irish Oatmeal offers a gluten-free option). It will just take a little longer to cook (4 minutes at high pressure, then release pressure naturally for 15 minutes).

PEACHES AND CREAM PORRIDGE

VEGETARIAN | 5 OR FEWER INGREDIENTS | ONE-POT | QUICK

Farina, or milled wheat, is a great way to get some iron into your diet, so if you have iron-poor blood (anemia), this recipe is a good choice for you. (Your heart has to work harder to pump blood and oxygen throughout the body when your iron levels are low.) Made with dates, peaches, and pistachios, this creamy dish packs in quite a bit of flavor.

Serves 4
Prep time: 5 minutes
Sauté: 7 minutes
Total time: 12 minutes

3 cups low-fat
   milk, divided
8 small dates, pitted
   and chopped
1 tablespoon shelled
   pistachios
6 tablespoons farina
1 cup canned unsweetened
   sliced peaches, drained
Ground cinnamon
   (optional)

PER SERVING: Calories 214, Total Fat 3g, Saturated Fat 1.3g, Cholesterol 9mg, Sodium 126mg, Potassium 495mg, Magnesium 41mg, Carbohydrates 40g, Sugars 25g, Added Sugars 0g, Fiber 3g, Protein 9g, Vitamin K 3mcg

1. Select Sauté. In the inner pot, combine 2 cups of milk, the dates, and the pistachios and stir together. Cook until the mixture comes to a boil, about 5 minutes, then, while whisking continuously, slowly add the farina, 1 tablespoon at a time, and whisk for about 1 minute, until it starts to thicken. Press Cancel.

2. Add the peaches and cover the pot (without sealing the lid). Let stand for 1 to 2 minutes, until the porridge is thick and creamy.

3. Divide the porridge among four bowls and top each with ¼ cup of the remaining milk and a pinch of cinnamon, if desired.

Substitution Tip: To make this dish dairy-free, swap out the milk for unsweetened plant-based milk.

CARROT CAKE BREAKFAST PORRIDGE

DAIRY-FREE | GLUTEN-FREE | VEGAN | ONE-POT

Made with carrots, walnuts, dates, and pumpkin pie spice, this porridge has carrot cake appeal. Walnuts supply heart-healthy omega-3s, which may help decrease triglycerides and slightly lower your blood pressure. While this dish takes longer to cook than traditional oatmeal, its hearty, chewy texture is worth the wait.

Serves 4
Prep time: 5 minutes
Cook time: 2 minutes at high pressure
Pressure release: Natural for 20 minutes, then Quick
Total time: 32 minutes

1 cup unsweetened soy milk

1 cup water

1 cup gluten-free oat groats (steel-cut or Irish oats)

1 medium banana, sliced

1 cup shredded carrots

8 small dates, pitted and thinly sliced

¼ cup unsweetened coconut flakes

½ teaspoon vanilla extract

⅓ cup chopped walnuts

1 teaspoon pumpkin pie spice

1. In the Instant Pot, combine the soy milk, water, oat groats, banana, carrots, dates, coconut, vanilla, and walnuts.

2. Lock the lid into place. Select Pressure Cook and cook on high pressure for 2 minutes. When the cooking is complete, allow the pressure to release naturally for 20 minutes, then quick release any remaining pressure and remove the lid.

3. Spoon the porridge into bowls, sprinkle with pumpkin spice, and serve.

Substitution Tip: If you don't have dates, you can use 2½ tablespoons of maple syrup instead. It will bump the dish to 7 grams of added sugars per serving, but that is still within heart-healthy limits. If you don't have pumpkin pie spice, you can use ½ teaspoon each of ground cinnamon and ground allspice.

PER SERVING (⅔ CUP): Calories 313, Total Fat 13g, Saturated Fat 3g, Cholesterol 36mg, Sodium 36mg, Potassium 464mg, Magnesium 45mg, Carbohydrates 45g, Sugars 15g, Added Sugars 0g, Fiber 8g, Protein 9g, Vitamin K 5mcg

STEAMED ASPARAGUS WITH RICOTTA, PAGE 40

CHAPTER 3

SALADS, STARTERS, AND SIDES

BEET AND FENNEL SALAD

GLUTEN-FREE | VEGETARIAN | ONE-POT

This simple beet combo with fennel and lemon makes quite a splash with sweet and tangy flavor notes. Beets are also rich in nitrates, anti-inflammatory substances that remove toxins from your bloodstream.

Serves 4
Prep time: 5 minutes
Cook time: 20 minutes at high pressure
Pressure release: Natural for 10 minutes, then Quick
Total time: 40 minutes

1½ cups water

2 large beets, scrubbed and dried

Nonstick cooking spray

1 small fennel bulb, sliced (about 1 cup)

1 tablespoon balsamic vinegar

1 tablespoon honey

Juice of ½ lemon

2 cups baby arugula

2 ounces feta cheese, crumbled

Freshly ground black pepper (optional)

PER SERVING: Calories 147, Total Fat 9.5g, Saturated Fat 3g, Cholesterol 13mg, Sodium 226mg, Potassium 344mg, Magnesium 27mg, Carbohydrates 14g, Sugars 11g, Added Sugars 4g, Fiber 2g, Protein 4g, Vitamin K 29mcg

1 Pour 1½ cups of water into the Instant Pot and set the trivet in the center.

2 Lightly coat each beet with nonstick spray. Wrap each tightly in aluminum foil and place on the trivet.

3 Lock the lid into place. Select Pressure Cook and cook on high pressure for 20 minutes. When the cooking is complete, allow the pressure to release naturally for 10 minutes, then quick release any remaining pressure and remove the lid.

4 Carefully remove the beets from the pot and let cool for 20 minutes. Unwrap each beet, using the foil and the pressure of your fingertips to peel the skin away and reveal the shiny beet flesh.

5 Chop the beets into ½-inch cubes (you should have about 1½ cups) and place in a medium bowl. Add the fennel, vinegar, honey, and lemon juice and toss until completed coated. Gently fold in the arugula and top with the feta. Season with pepper (if using)

6 Divide evenly among four small plates and serve.

Substitution Tip: To make this dairy-free, swap out the feta for 3 tablespoons of chopped walnuts.

HONEY-GLAZED CARROTS

**DAIRY-FREE | GLUTEN-FREE | VEGETARIAN | 5 OR FEWER INGREDIENTS
ONE-POT | QUICK**

Carrots and honey are a classic combo, and when cooked in the Instant Pot, the carrots' caramelized finish surely meets expectations. The carrots stay al dente while the honey flavor infuses them, making this dish a sweet, heart-healthy option. A little honey goes a long way, keeping it low in added sugars—but high in taste.

Serves 4
Prep time: 4 minutes
Cook time: 2 minutes at high pressure
Pressure release: Quick
Sauté: 2 minutes
Total time: 13 minutes

1 cup water
1 pound carrots, sliced
1 tablespoon olive oil
⅛ teaspoon salt
1 tablespoon honey
¼ teaspoon dried rosemary

PER SERVING: Calories 102, Total Fat 4g, Saturated Fat 0.5g, Cholesterol 0mg, Sodium 168mg, Potassium 437mg, Magnesium 17mg, Carbohydrates 17g, Sugars 11g, Added Sugars 4g, Fiber 4g, Protein 1g, Vitamin K 13mcg

1 Pour 1 cup of water into the Instant Pot and set the trivet in the center.

2 Cut a piece of aluminum foil to fit over the trivet and set it on the trivet. Place the carrots on top.

3 Lock the lid into place. Select Pressure Cook and cook on high pressure for 2 minutes. When the cooking is complete, quick release the pressure and remove the lid.

4 Carefully remove the carrots. Turn off the Instant Pot and drain the water from the inner pot.

5 Return the inner liner to the Instant Pot. Combine the oil, salt, honey, and rosemary in the pot. Select Sauté and heat for 1 to 2 minutes, until the oil starts to shimmer. Press Cancel.

6 Return the carrots to the Instant Pot and toss with the honey mixture until well coated. Serve.

Flavor Boost: To add a tangy kick to the dish, add a splash of aged balsamic vinegar.

SPINACH AND MUSHROOM SALAD

**DAIRY-FREE | GLUTEN-FREE | VEGAN | 5 OR FEWER INGREDIENTS
ONE-POT | QUICK**

Mushrooms pack in vitamin D, which promotes heart health by supporting the lining of your blood vessels so blood flows smoothly throughout the body. Vitamin D also helps protect your bones. In this recipe, nutrient-dense mushrooms are complemented by the bright flavors of mustard and vinegar.

Serves 4
Prep time: 2 minutes
Sauté: 5 minutes
Total time: 7 minutes

2 tablespoons olive oil

1 pound white mushrooms, rinsed well and sliced

2 tablespoons balsamic vinegar

2 teaspoons Dijon mustard

½ teaspoon dried basil

4 cups baby spinach

PER SERVING (ABOUT ½ CUP):
Calories 102, Total Fat 7g,
Saturated Fat 1g, Cholesterol
0mg, Sodium 90mg, Potassium
538mg, Magnesium 36mg,
Carbohydrates 7g, Sugars 4g,
Added Sugars 0g, Fiber 2g,
Protein 5g, Vitamin K 152mcg

1 Select Sauté and wait 30 seconds for the Instant Pot to warm. Add the oil, mushrooms, vinegar, mustard, and basil and stir to coat well. Sauté for 4 to 5 minutes, until the mushrooms have cooked down.

2 Press Cancel. Add the spinach and give it a good stir for 1 to 2 minutes. The residual heat should wilt the spinach.

3 Serve warm.

Variation Tip: For an even earthier flavor, swap out the white mushrooms for creminis. Garnish with thin strips of radicchio to balance the overall flavors with its slightly bitter yet floral notes.

BLISTERED SNAP PEAS WITH YOGURT CHEESE

GLUTEN-FREE | VEGETARIAN | QUICK

This dish combines the irresistible flavors of feta and za'atar, a Middle East-ern spice blend made with thyme, lemon, and sesame seeds. Homemade yogurt cheese keeps it low in saturated fat.

Serves 4
Prep time: 5 minutes
Sauté: 6 minutes
Cook time: 2 minutes at high pressure
Pressure release: Natural for 5 minutes, then Quick
Total time: 23 minutes

1 tablespoon olive oil

8 ounces fresh snap peas

1½ cups water

½ cup plain low-fat Greek yogurt

2 ounces feta cheese, crumbled

1 teaspoon low-sodium soy sauce

¼ teaspoon garlic powder

1 teaspoon chopped fresh mint, for garnish

1 teaspoon za'atar, for garnish

Freshly ground black pepper (optional)

PER SERVING: Calories 117, Total Fat 7g, Saturated Fat 3g, Cholesterol 15mg, Sodium 223mg, Potassium 56mg, Magnesium 8mg, Carbohydrates 6g, Sugars 4g, Added Sugars 0g, Fiber 2g, Protein 7g, Vitamin K 16mcg

1 Select Sauté and wait 30 seconds for the Instant Pot to warm. Pour in the oil and heat for 30 seconds, until it starts to sizzle. Add the snap peas and sauté for 2 to 3 minutes, until browned on one side. Stir well, then cook for 2 minutes more. Transfer the snap peas to a medium bowl and set aside.

2 Immediately pour 1½ cups of water into the Instant Pot and set the trivet in the center.

3 In a small bowl, combine the yogurt, feta, soy sauce, and garlic powder. Transfer the mixture to a 6-inch round cake pan and place the pan on top of the trivet.

4 Lock the lid into place. Select Pressure Cook and cook on high pressure for 2 minutes. When the cooking is complete, allow the pressure to release naturally for 5 minutes, then quick release any remaining pressure and remove the lid.

5 Use a slotted spoon to remove the yogurt cheese from the pot, allowing any liquid that has formed to drain, and layer the yogurt cheese onto the snap peas.

6 Garnish with the mint and za'atar and season with pepper, if desired, before serving.

STEAMED ASPARAGUS WITH RICOTTA

GLUTEN-FREE | VEGETARIAN | 5 OR FEWER INGREDIENTS | ONE-POT QUICK

Asparagus supports healthy blood pressure, and its amino acid, asparagine, helps flush your body of excess salt. In this recipe, the asparagus is lightly steamed (to give a nice al dente bite) and topped with a delicious blend of ricotta, herbs, and lemony essence from the za'atar. To keep the asparagus from going limp, you won't want to build up pressure in your pot (not even just for a 1-minute cooking time). The key is to steam them over boiling water for just a few minutes.

Serves 4
Prep time: 2 minutes
Steam: 10 minutes
Total time: 12 minutes

1½ cups water

1 pound asparagus, trimmed

½ cup ricotta cheese

1 teaspoon za'atar

1½ teaspoons olive oil

PER SERVING: Calories 98, Total Fat 6g, Saturated Fat 2g, Cholesterol 15mg, Sodium 50mg, Potassium 296mg, Magnesium 22mg, Carbohydrates 8g, Sugars 3g, Added Sugars 0g, Fiber 3g, Protein 5g, Vitamin K 49mcg

1 Pour 1½ cups of water into the Instant Pot and set the trivet in the center. Select Sauté and bring the water to a boil, about 5 minutes.

2 Using tongs, carefully layer the asparagus on the trivet, arranging the top layer of asparagus perpendicular to the bottom layer.

3 Cover the Instant Pot with a clean kitchen towel and steam for 4 to 5 minutes, until the asparagus reaches your desired tenderness.

4 Press Cancel. Transfer the asparagus to a plate.

5 Top with dollops of ricotta, distributing them as evenly as you can. Sprinkle with the za'atar, drizzle with the olive oil, and serve.

Ingredient Tip: Za'atar can be found at Trader Joe's and specialty markets, as well as online. If you can't find any at your local grocery store, you can mix equal parts dried oregano, dried thyme, sesame seeds, and grated lemon zest to create your own.

BROCCOLI BITES WITH CHEDDAR

VEGETARIAN

With a base of broccoli and sweet potato, this recipe offers plenty of nutrients, including calcium, potassium, and vitamin A. It all comes together with eggs, a bit of cheese, some bread crumbs, and a touch of soy sauce—simple, common ingredients you likely already have.

Makes 7 bites
Prep time: 5 minutes
Cook time: 12 minutes at high pressure
Pressure release: Natural for 10 minutes, then Quick
Total time: 32 minutes

1½ cups water

Nonstick cooking spray

1½ cups chopped broccoli florets

½ cup grated peeled sweet potato

2 medium eggs

1½ teaspoons potato starch

1 ounce low-fat cheddar cheese, grated

1 teaspoon low-sodium soy sauce

3 tablespoons panko bread crumbs

PER SERVING (2 BROCCOLI BITES): Calories 125, Total Fat 3g, Saturated Fat 1g, Cholesterol 96mg, Sodium 194mg, Potassium 273mg, Magnesium 21mg, Carbohydrates 17g, Sugars 13g, Added Sugars 0g, Fiber 2g, Protein 7g, Vitamin K 32mcg

1 Pour 1½ cups of water into the Instant Pot and set the trivet in the center. Coat a 7-cup silicone egg mold with nonstick spray.

2 In a medium bowl, combine the broccoli, sweet potato, eggs, potato starch, cheese, soy sauce, and bread crumbs. Scoop and press the batter firmly into each egg mold, so that each well is about half to two-thirds full. Place the egg mold on top of the trivet.

3 Lock the lid into place. Select Pressure Cook and cook on high pressure for 12 minutes. When the cooking is complete, allow the pressure to release naturally for 10 minutes, then quick release any remaining pressure and remove the lid. Remove the egg mold.

4 With a large spoon, carefully remove the egg bites from the mold. Or wait 10 minutes until they are cool enough to pop out of the mold with your thumbs and forefingers.

5 Serve warm.

Variation Tip: To make this gluten-free, swap out the bread crumbs for an equal quantity of rolled oats.

SWEET PEA AND POTATO SALAD WITH YOGURT AND DILL

GLUTEN-FREE | VEGETARIAN | ONE-POT | QUICK

This recipe was inspired by one of my favorite picnic sides. It's a cool and refreshing combination of hearty vegetables, light yogurt, and zesty dill. Sweet peas are naturally high in fiber (both soluble and insoluble), low in fat, and cholesterol-free, making them a great heart-smart food choice.

Serves 6
Prep time: 10 minutes
Cook time: 5 minutes at high pressure
Pressure release: Natural for 10 minutes, then Quick
Total time: 30 minutes

1½ cups water

4 baby red potatoes, rinsed

3 cups frozen sweet peas, slightly thawed

½ cup plain low-fat Greek yogurt

2 tablespoons chopped fresh dill

½ teaspoon dried basil

Juice of 1 lemon

1 small radish, thinly sliced, for garnish

PER SERVING: Calories 148, Total Fat 1g, Saturated Fat 1g, Cholesterol 2.5mg, Sodium 123mg, Potassium 544mg, Magnesium 49mg, Carbohydrates 26g, Sugars 7g, Added Sugars 0g, Fiber 6g, Protein 9g, Vitamin K 30mcg

1 Pour 1½ cups of water into the Instant Pot and set the trivet in the center. Place the potatoes directly on the trivet.

2 Lock the lid into place. Select Pressure Cook and cook on high pressure for 5 minutes. When the cooking is complete, allow the pressure to release naturally for 10 minutes, then quick release any remaining pressure and remove the lid.

3 Carefully transfer the potatoes to a wire rack to cool completely.

4 In a medium bowl, combine the sweet peas, yogurt, dill, basil, and lemon juice.

5 Cube the cooled potatoes and gently fold them into the yogurt mixture. Garnish with the radish and serve.

Variation Tip: If you want to try something a little different, swap out the baby red potatoes for 4 medium carrots instead. Cook them using the same method and time, let them cool, and then chop them into small rounds.

CREAMED SPINACH

VEGETARIAN | ONE-POT

The homemade cream of mushroom soup keeps this dish lower in sodium than typical creamed spinach dishes. With a hefty dose of spinach, you'll get heart-healthy nutrients including several B vitamins (B_2, B_6, and folate), and iron, which transports oxygen through your bloodstream.

Serves 6
Prep time: 5 minutes
Sauté: 8 minutes
Cook time: 2 minutes at high pressure
Pressure release: Natural for 5 minutes, then Quick
Total time: 41 minutes (including time to make the soup)

1 tablespoon avocado oil

½ medium yellow onion, chopped

2 cups Cream of Mushroom Soup (page 125)

¼ cup low-fat milk

10 ounces frozen spinach

½ teaspoon ground nutmeg

PER SERVING: Calories 166, Total Fat 8g, Saturated Fat 1.5g, Cholesterol 4mg, Sodium 200mg, Potassium 413mg, Magnesium 21mg, Carbohydrates 15g, Sugars 7g, Added Sugars 0g, Fiber 2g, Protein 8g, Vitamin K 8mcg

1 Select Sauté and wait for 30 seconds for the Instant Pot to warm. Pour in the oil and heat for 30 seconds, until it starts to sizzle. Add the onion and sauté, stirring occasionally, for 6 minutes, or until softened. Press Cancel.

2 Add the cream of mushroom soup, milk, spinach, and nutmeg.

3 Lock the lid into place. Select Pressure Cook and cook on high pressure for 2 minutes. When the cooking is complete, allow the pressure to release naturally for 5 minutes, then quick release any remaining pressure and remove the lid.

4 Serve warm.

Flavor Boost: To add a little natural sweetness and some contrasting color, sauté ½ cup of chopped red bell pepper with the onion.

DEVILED EGG BITES

Preparing these eggs in a mold versus traditional boiling keeps the creamy appeal of deviled eggs without the messy, time-consuming task of peeling them. Egg yolks support heart health, as they are a rich source of B vitamins, providing nearly half of your daily requirement for vitamin B_{12}.

Serves 6
Prep time: 3 minutes
Cook time: 8 minutes at high pressure
Pressure release: Natural for 10 minutes, then Quick
Total time: 26 minutes

1½ cups water
Nonstick cooking spray
6 medium eggs
¼ cup plain low-fat Greek yogurt
1 teaspoon Dijon mustard
1 tablespoon avocado oil
¼ teaspoon garlic powder
1 teaspoon fresh lemon juice
Paprika, for garnish (optional)

PER SERVING (1 DEVILED EGG): Calories 98, Total Fat 7g, Saturated Fat 2g, Cholesterol 165mg, Sodium 78mg, Potassium 76mg, Magnesium 7mg, Carbohydrates 1g, Sugars 1g, Added Sugars 0g, Fiber 0g, Protein 7g, Vitamin K 2mcg

1 Pour 1½ cups of water into the Instant Pot and set the trivet in the center.

2 Coat a 7-cup silicone egg mold with nonstick spray. Carefully crack an egg into each well (you'll have one empty well; egg molds generally have 7 wells). Cover the mold with its lid or aluminum foil. Place the egg mold on the trivet.

3 Lock the lid into place. Select Pressure Cook and cook on high pressure for 8 minutes. When the cooking is complete, allow the pressure to release naturally for 10 minutes, then quick release any remaining pressure and remove the lid.

4 Using a small spoon, carefully transfer the center yolk from each egg bite into a small bowl. Try to keep the bottoms of the egg whites intact. Transfer the egg whites to a plate.

5 Mash the yolks with a fork. Mix in the yogurt, mustard, oil, garlic powder, and lemon juice until well combined and creamy.

6 Divide the yolk mixture evenly among the egg whites. Garnish with a sprinkling of paprika, if desired, and serve.

Flavor Boost: To brighten the flavor, garnish with some grated lemon zest.

STEAMED BUNS WITH SWEET BEAN FILLING

DAIRY-FREE | VEGAN | WORTH THE WAIT

Steamed buns are perfect for cooking in the Instant Pot. These treats use the bun recipe from chapter 8; the yeasty bun itself requires few ingredients, but the dough does require some care and time. Instead of a sugar-sweetened filling, the date-sweetened bean filling contains no added sugars and only whole-food ingredients. Beans support your heart with soluble fiber for cholesterol control and potassium to help keep blood pressure in check.

Makes 15 buns
Prep time: 15 minutes, plus 2 hours rising time
Sauté: 35 minutes
Total time: 2 hours 40 minutes (including time to make the buns)

1 batch Steamed Bun dough (page 122)
¾ cup low-sodium canned black beans, drained and rinsed
7 small pitted dates
1 tablespoon oil
1½ tablespoons water
1½ cups water
Nonstick cooking spray

PER SERVING (1 FILLED BUN):
Calories 101, Total Fat 2g, Saturated Fat 0.3g, Cholesterol 0mg, Sodium 63mg, Potassium 77mg, Magnesium 10mg, Carbohydrates 18g, Sugars 3g, Added Sugars 1g, Fiber 2g, Protein 3g, Vitamin K 2mcg

1   Prepare the bun dough through step 5 as directed on page 122.

2   In a food processor, combine the beans, dates, oil, and water and process for 1 to 2 minutes, until smooth.

3   Create a well in each ball of dough with your thumbs and scoop 1 rounded teaspoon of the bean mixture into each. Form the dough back into a ball, enclosing the bean paste as fully as possible.

4   Pour 1½ cups of water into the Instant Pot and set the trivet in the center. Select Sauté and bring the water to a boil, about 6 minutes.

5   Turn a 6-inch round cake pan upside-down and coat with nonstick spray. Working in batches, place the 4 buns, evenly separated, onto the upside-down cake pan. Carefully place the pan on top of the trivet. Cover the Instant Pot with a clean kitchen towel and steam for 7 to 8 minutes, until the buns are fluffy. Transfer the buns to a wire rack. Repeat three more times to steam the remaining buns.

Variation Tip: Black beans work well in this recipe, but you can vary the filling by using chickpeas or kidney beans.

SPRING ROLLS WITH SEASONED GROUND PORK

DAIRY-FREE | ONE-POT | QUICK

Seasoned ground pork paired with refreshing carrots, cucumber, and cilantro makes this dish a tantalizing—and antioxidant-rich—choice for your taste buds. Limiting the pork to 2 ounces per serving keeps this dish low in saturated fat, while still packing in the flavor.

Serves 4
Prep time: 10 minutes
Sauté: 7 minutes
Total time: 17 minutes

2 teaspoons toasted sesame oil, divided

½ medium Vidalia onion, chopped

8 ounces 80% lean ground pork

1 teaspoon crushed garlic

1 teaspoon grated fresh ginger

3 teaspoons low-sodium soy sauce, divided

1 cup shredded carrots

½ medium cucumber, peeled and cut into thin 4-inch-long strips

3 tablespoons coarsely chopped fresh cilantro

3 tablespoons coarsely chopped fresh mint

3 tablespoons sliced scallion (green part only)

1 tablespoon unseasoned rice vinegar

1 teaspoon honey

4 rice paper wrappers or small crisp romaine lettuce leaves

1 cup water

1. Select Sauté and wait 30 seconds for the Instant Pot to warm. Pour in 1 teaspoon of sesame oil and heat for 30 seconds, until it starts to sizzle. Add the onion and ground pork. Break up the meat with a spatula and cook, stirring occasionally, for about 5 minutes, until the pork is cooked through. Add the garlic and ginger and cook for 1 minute more. Press Cancel.

2. Transfer the seasoned pork to a bowl. Mix in 1 teaspoon of soy sauce.

3. Place the carrots and cucumber in separate small bowls. In a third small bowl, combine the cilantro, mint, and scallion. In a small cup, mix together the remaining 2 teaspoons of soy sauce, the vinegar, and the honey. Fill a medium bowl with 1 cup of warm water.

PER SERVING (1 WRAP): Calories 133, Total Fat 9g, Saturated Fat 2.5g, Cholesterol 20mg, Sodium 215mg, Potassium 133mg, Magnesium 13mg, Carbohydrates 10g, Sugars 5g, Added Sugars 1g, Fiber 1g, Protein 6g, Vitamin K 15mcg

4   For each spring roll, dip a rice paper wrapper in the water for 10 to 15 seconds, until softened (not soggy). (If using a romaine leaf, you can skip this.) Lay the wrapper flat and top with some of the seasoned pork, carrots, cucumber, cilantro, mint, and scallions, dividing them evenly among the wraps. Drizzle each with 1 to 2 teaspoons of the prepared sauce. Fold in the sides of each wrapper, then roll up snugly to enclose the filling and serve.

Flavor Boost: For a little heat, add a pinch of red pepper flakes to the seasoned pork before filling the wraps.

TOFU AND VEGGIE "RAMEN" WITH SOBA NOODLES, PAGE 60

— CHAPTER 4 —
MEATLESS MAINS

LENTIL CURRY

DAIRY-FREE | VEGAN | ONE-POT

This lentil curry is aromatic and hearty. The lentil base delivers protein, fiber, and heart-healthy B vitamins. Because lentils are starchy, this dish is balanced out with just a bit of chopped potatoes and some nonstarchy carrots that provide antioxidants, including beta-carotene, which supports your eye and skin health.

Serves 6
Prep time: 5 minutes
Sauté: 6 minutes
Cook time: 4 minutes at high pressure
Pressure release: Natural for 20 minutes, then Quick
Total time: 40 minutes

2 teaspoons olive oil

½ medium yellow onion, chopped

1 large red bell pepper, chopped

2 cups water

1 teaspoon ground cumin

1 teaspoon crushed garlic

½ teaspoon chili powder

1 tablespoon curry powder or garam masala

1 tablespoon low-sodium soy sauce

2 medium carrots, chopped

4 small Yukon Gold potatoes, chopped

1 cup dried red lentils

1 cup low-sodium marinara sauce

1 Select Sauté and wait 30 seconds for the Instant Pot to warm. Pour in the oil and heat for 30 seconds, until it starts to sizzle. Add the onion and bell pepper and sauté for 5 minutes, or until the veggies start to soften (add 1 to 2 tablespoons of water if the veggies start to stick).

2 Add the water, cumin, garlic, chili powder, curry powder, soy sauce, carrots, potatoes, lentils, and marinara and stir.

3 Lock the lid into place. Select Pressure Cook and cook on high pressure for 4 minutes. When the cooking is complete, allow the pressure to release naturally for 20 minutes, then quick release any remaining pressure and remove the lid. Serve warm.

Variation Tip: If you have some Zesty Carrot Tomato Sauce (page 119) on hand, you can replace the marinara with an equal amount.

PER SERVING (1 CUP): Calories 243, Total Fat 3g, Saturated Fat 1g, Cholesterol 0mg, Sodium 154mg, Potassium 1,025mg, Magnesium 62mg, Carbohydrates 46g, Sugars 4g, Added Sugars 0g, Fiber 8g, Protein 11g, Vitamin K 5mcg

VEGAN CHICKPEA CHILI

DAIRY-FREE | VEGAN | ONE-POT

Homemade carrot tomato sauce contributes to the veggie richness of this chili with the addition of bell peppers and carrots to the tomato base. If you prepare the sauce a night or two ahead of time, this dish will take less than 15 minutes to prepare. Or, you can use an equal amount of low-sodium tomato sauce instead. Silver Palate is an ideal brand because its marinara has less than 200 milligrams sodium per ½-cup serving and has a nice balance of acidity and zest.

Serves 4
Prep time: 5 minutes
Cook time: 1 minute at high pressure
Pressure release: Quick
Total time: 37 minutes (including time to make the sauce)

4 cups Zesty Carrot Tomato Sauce (page 119)
1 (14.5-ounce) can low-sodium chickpeas, drained and rinsed
½ cup dried red lentils
1 tablespoon ground cumin
4 loose cups baby spinach
Red pepper flakes (optional)

PER SERVING (1 CUP): Calories 303, Total Fat 5g, Saturated Fat 1g, Cholesterol 0mg, Sodium 405mg, Potassium 1,479mg, Magnesium 78mg, Carbohydrates 52g, Sugars 14g, Added Sugars 0g, Fiber 15g, Protein 15g, Vitamin K 169mcg

1 Pour the tomato sauce into the Instant Pot and add the chickpeas, lentils, cumin, and baby spinach. Stir to combine.

2 Lock the lid into place. Select Pressure Cook and cook on high pressure for 1 minute. When the cooking is complete, quick release the pressure and remove the lid.

3 Garnish with red pepper flakes, if desired, and serve.

Variation Tip: If you prefer, you can swap out the spinach for another large red or orange bell pepper (diced), as you'll already use one in the carrot tomato sauce recipe.

CRUSTLESS FETA AND MUSHROOM QUICHE

VEGETARIAN | WORTH THE WAIT

Traditional quiche crusts are loaded with saturated fat from butter or lard. To lower the saturated fat, we go crust-free by using cubes of toasted whole wheat bread instead. The bread soaks up the flavors and adds a fun texture.

Serves 4
Prep time: 15 minutes
Cook time: 30 minutes at high pressure
Pressure release: Natural for 10 minutes, then Quick
Total time: 1 hour

Nonstick cooking spray

1½ cups water

1½ ounces feta cheese, divided

4 medium eggs

½ cup low-fat cottage cheese

⅛ teaspoon salt

2 garlic cloves, crushed

1 teaspoon Italian seasoning

1 cup chopped mushrooms

1 cup baby spinach

1 slice whole wheat bread, toasted and cut into ½-inch pieces

¼ cup chopped fresh basil

1. Coat a 6-inch high-sided springform cake pan with nonstick spray.

2. Pour 1½ cups of water into the Instant Pot and set the trivet in the center.

3. Fold an 18-inch sheet of aluminum foil lengthwise into thirds so it forms a 4-inch-wide strip. Place the foil strip over the trivet so the ends overhang the trivet evenly (this will make it easier to remove the pan from the Instant Pot after cooking).

4. Set aside 1 tablespoon of feta for garnish. In a medium bowl, mix together the eggs, cottage cheese, salt, garlic, Italian seasoning, remaining feta, mushrooms, spinach, and toast pieces.

5. Pour the egg mixture into the prepared cake pan and cover tightly with aluminum foil. Set the pan over the foil strip on the trivet and fold the ends of the strip over the pan so you can close the lid.

PER SERVING: Calories 152, Total Fat 8g, Saturated Fat 3g, Cholesterol 174mg, Sodium 312mg, Potassium 257mg, Magnesium 26mg, Carbohydrates 8g, Sugars 3g, Added Sugars 0g, Fiber 1g, Protein 12g, Vitamin K 53mcg

6   Lock the lid into place. Select Pressure Cook and cook on high pressure for 30 minutes. When the cooking is complete, allow the pressure to release naturally for 10 minutes, then quick release any remaining pressure and remove the lid.

7   Remove the pan using the ends of the foil strip and let cool for 5 minutes.

8   Garnish the quiche with the basil and reserved 1 tablespoon of feta. Unlatch the springform ring and gently lift it off. Slice the quiche into quarters and carefully use a small spatula to transfer one wedge to each plate, then serve.

VEGETARIAN "FRIED" RICE

DAIRY-FREE | VEGETARIAN | ONE-POT | QUICK

This rice is prepared using a couple of different cooking methods, all in the same pot. A combo of low-sodium chicken broth, water, and some low-sodium soy sauce keeps the salt content much lower than traditional fried rice, making this a heart-smart option.

Serves 6
Prep time: 5 minutes
Sauté: 4 minutes
Cook time: 3 minutes at high pressure
Pressure release: Natural for 10 minutes, then Quick
Total time: 27 minutes

2 teaspoons olive oil

2 medium eggs, whisked

2 garlic cloves, minced

¾ cup low-sodium chicken broth

¾ cup water

1 cup uncooked jasmine rice

1½ cups frozen peas and carrots

2 tablespoons low-sodium soy sauce

1 teaspoon toasted sesame oil

1 teaspoon grated fresh ginger

¼ cup sliced almonds, for garnish

2 to 3 tablespoons chopped scallion (green part only), for garnish

1 Select Sauté and wait 30 seconds for the Instant Pot to warm. Pour in the olive oil and heat for 30 seconds, until it sizzles. Add the eggs and use a silicone spatula to push them around until they are set, 1½ to 2 minutes. Transfer the eggs to a plate and set aside. Press Cancel.

2 While the inner pot is still warm, add the garlic and toss it around for 30 seconds, then add the broth, water, rice, and frozen veggies.

3 Lock the lid into place. Select Pressure Cook and cook on high pressure for 3 minutes. When the cooking is complete, allow the pressure to release naturally for 10 minutes, then quick release any remaining pressure and remove the lid.

4 Mix in the soy sauce, sesame oil, and ginger until well combined. Toss in the scrambled eggs. Garnish with the sliced almonds and scallion and serve.

PER SERVING: Calories 210, Total Fat 7g, Saturated Fat 1g, Cholesterol 55mg, Sodium 268mg, Potassium 143mg, Magnesium 27mg, Carbohydrates 31g, Sugars 2g, Added Sugars 0g, Fiber 2g, Protein 7g, Vitamin K 5mcg

ZUCCHINI AND PITA "FRITTATA"

VEGETARIAN | 5 OR FEWER INGREDIENTS | WORTH THE WAIT

Za'atar is a flavorful Middle Eastern spice mix with the essence of lemon, thyme, and sesame. The layers of seasoned eggs and cottage cheese, pita, and zucchini infused with the fragrant za'atar cook up beautifully.

Serves 4
Prep time: 5 minutes
Cook time: 30 minutes at high pressure
Pressure release: Natural for 15 minutes, then Quick
Total time: 1 hour 5 minutes (including resting time)

1½ cups water
Nonstick cooking spray
4 medium eggs, lightly beaten
1 cup cottage cheese
2 tablespoons za'atar
2 (6-inch) whole wheat pitas, cut into 4 wedges each
1 medium zucchini, sliced

PER SERVING: Calories 285, Total Fat 8g, Saturated Fat 3g, Cholesterol 172mg, Sodium 502mg, Potassium 345mg, Magnesium 53mg, Carbohydrates 38g, Sugars 5g, Added Sugars 1g, Fiber 5g, Protein 18g, Vitamin K 3mcg

Variation Tip: If you don't have za'atar, you can use Italian seasoning or any favorite seasoning blend.

1. Pour 1½ cups of water into the Instant Pot and set the trivet in the center. Fold an 18-inch sheet of aluminum foil lengthwise into thirds so it forms a 4-inch-wide strip. Place the foil strip over the trivet so the ends overhang the trivet evenly (this will make it easier to remove the cake pans from the Instant Pot after cooking).

2. Coat two 6-inch round cake pans with non-stick spray.

3. In a medium bowl, mix the eggs, cottage cheese, and za'atar. Layer each cake pan with one-quarter of the egg mixture, 4 wedges of pita and one-quarter of the zucchini; then repeat with a second layer of each for each cake pan. Tightly cover the pans with aluminum foil.

4. Stack the pans over the foil strip on the trivet and fold the ends of the strip over the pans so you'll be able to close the lid.

5. Lock the lid into place. Select Pressure Cook and cook on high pressure for 30 minutes. When the cooking is complete, allow the pressure to release naturally for 15 minutes, then quick release any remaining pressure and remove the lid.

6. Remove the pans and the foil and let the frittatas rest for 10 minutes before serving.

SAVORY TAMALE PIE

VEGETARIAN | WORTH THE WAIT

This starchy delight combines the goodness of seasoned black beans, cruciferous Brussels sprouts, and a cornmeal topping that's low in fat and added sugar.

Serves 4
Prep time: 10 minutes
Cook time: 25 minutes at high pressure
Pressure release: Natural for 5 minutes, then Quick
Total time: 45 minutes

FOR THE CORN BREAD TOPPING

¼ cup cornmeal

½ cup low-fat buttermilk

1 medium egg

1 tablespoon olive oil

1 tablespoon honey

½ cup all-purpose flour

½ teaspoon baking soda

⅛ teaspoon salt

1½ cups water

FOR THE PIE FILLING

Nonstick cooking spray

1½ cups low-sodium canned black beans, drained and rinsed

1 teaspoon ground cumin

1 teaspoon garlic powder

½ teaspoon chili powder or smoked paprika

⅛ teaspoon salt

1 teaspoon olive oil

TO MAKE THE CORN BREAD TOPPING

1   In a medium bowl, combine the cornmeal, buttermilk, egg, oil, and honey. Mix in the flour, baking soda, and salt. Set the batter aside.

TO MAKE THE PIE FILLING

2   Pour 1½ cups of water into the Instant Pot and set the trivet in the center. Coat 4 (8-ounce) ramekins with nonstick spray. Lightly coat 4 small squares of aluminum foil with nonstick spray.

3   In a medium bowl, stir together the black beans, cumin, garlic powder, chili powder, salt, and olive oil.

4   Layer each ramekin with ½ cup of the Brussels sprouts and ⅓ cup of the bean mixture, then top with ¼ cup of the corn bread batter. Use a spatula to carefully spread the batter over the beans. Wrap each ramekin tightly with the prepared foil squares, coated-side down, and place on the trivet.

FOR THE PIE FILLING (cont)

2 cups small Brussels
   sprouts, halved
¼ cup plain low-fat
   Greek yogurt
4 teaspoons low-sodium,
   low-sugar ketchup

PER SERVING (1 RAMEKIN):
Calories 259, Total Fat 7g,
Saturated Fat 1g, Cholesterol
43mg, Sodium 402mg,
Potassium 576mg, Magnesium
58mg, Carbohydrates 41g,
Sugars 10g, Added Sugars
4g, Fiber 7g, Protein 10g,
Vitamin K 8mcg

5 Lock the lid into place. Select Pressure Cook and cook on high pressure for 25 minutes. When the cooking is complete, allow the pressure to release naturally for 5 minutes, then quick release any remaining pressure and remove the lid.

6 Carefully remove the foil from each ramekin. Garnish each with 1 tablespoon of yogurt and a drizzle of ketchup and serve.

CHICKPEA AND LENTIL RATATOUILLE

DAIRY-FREE | VEGETARIAN | ONE-POT | WORTH THE WAIT

If you prepare the ratatouille base ahead of time, this dish will only take 15 minutes from start to finish. I like to prepare the base the night before to save time. What's heart-smart about this dish is that it uses little oil and is full of veggie goodness from the zesty infusion of eggplant, zucchini, tomatoes, pumpkin, and spices. The addition of spinach contributes iron and more fiber to the mix.

Serves 4
Prep time: 5 minutes
Cook time: 1 minute at high pressure
Pressure release: Quick
Total time: 51 minutes (including time to make the ratatouille base)

5 cups Ratatouille Base (page 120)

1 (14.5-ounce) can low-sodium chickpeas, drained and rinsed

½ cup dried red lentils

1 tablespoon ground cumin

2 cups baby spinach

PER SERVING: Calories 323, Total Fat 6g, Saturated Fat 1g, Cholesterol 0mg, Sodium 292mg, Potassium 1,430mg, Magnesium 118mg, Carbohydrates 57g, Sugars 18g, Added Sugars 1g, Fiber 16g, Protein 16g, Vitamin K 111mcg

1 Pour the ratatouille base into the Instant Pot. Add the chickpeas, lentils, cumin, and spinach and stir to combine.

2 Lock the lid into place. Select Pressure Cook and cook on high pressure for 1 minute. When the cooking is complete, quick release the pressure, remove the lid, and serve.

Flavor Boost: Garnish with a few pinches of red pepper flakes to bring some spicy warmth to the dish.

CORN, SPINACH, AND MUSHROOM SOUP

DAIRY-FREE | GLUTEN-FREE | ONE-POT | QUICK

This brothy soup is as nourishing as it is satisfying. The addition of beans for protein also lends the soup starch and amino acids to prevent muscle loss and improve your mood and sleep. Mushrooms are rich in B vitamins, including niacin, riboflavin, and pantothenic acid. According to a 2021 systemic review published in the American Journal of Medicine, *eating mushrooms may help reduce cholesterol and improve overall lipid profiles.*

Serves 4
Prep time: 5 minutes
Sauté: 11 minutes
Total time: 16 minutes

2 teaspoons olive oil

2 cups frozen corn kernels

1 teaspoon ground cumin

1 teaspoon garlic powder

½ teaspoon chili powder (optional)

8 ounces mushrooms, sliced

1 tablespoon white wine vinegar or rice vinegar

4 cups low-sodium chicken broth

1½ cups low-sodium black beans, drained and rinsed

⅛ teaspoon salt

4 cups baby spinach

PER SERVING: Calories 224, Total Fat 3g, Saturated Fat 1g, Cholesterol 0mg, Sodium 184mg, Potassium 1,022mg, Magnesium 91mg, Carbohydrates 40g, Sugars 5g, Added Sugars 0g, Fiber 10g, Protein 15g, Vitamin K 146mcg

1 Select Sauté and wait 30 seconds for the Instant Pot to warm. Pour in the oil and heat for 30 seconds, until it sizzles. Stir in the corn, cumin, garlic powder, and chili powder (if using). Sauté for 3 minutes, until fragrant, then add the mushrooms and vinegar and cook for 3 minutes more, until the mushrooms start to cook down.

2 Add the broth, beans, and salt and cook for 3 minutes more, until the mixture comes to a boil. Add the spinach, 1 cup at a time, and cook for 1 minute, until it is wilted.

3 Divide evenly among four bowls and serve.

Variation Tip: If you prefer a different protein, you can swap out the beans for an equal amount of tofu.

TOFU AND VEGGIE "RAMEN" WITH SOBA NOODLES

DAIRY-FREE | GLUTEN-FREE | VEGAN

With oodles of noodles, ramen is a comfort food classic, but the broth is usually high in sodium. This version uses veggies, garlic, ginger, and tamari to nicely infuse flavor into a homemade broth (an option that is much lower in sodium).

Serves 4
Prep time: 10 minutes
Sauté: 14 minutes
Cook time: 4 minutes at high pressure
Pressure release: Natural for 10 minutes, then Quick
Total time: 43 minutes

2 teaspoons olive oil

2 large red bell peppers, thinly sliced

1 cup coarsely chopped chard

1 cup chopped mushrooms

1 garlic clove, crushed

1 teaspoon grated fresh ginger

4 cups water

1 tablespoon low-sodium tamari

¼ cup frozen corn kernels

6 ounces soba noodles

1 pound firm tofu, cut into cubes

4 scallions (green parts only), chopped, for garnish

1 medium avocado, cubed

1. Select Sauté and wait 30 seconds for the Instant Pot to warm. Pour in the oil and heat for 30 seconds, until it sizzles. Add the bell peppers, chard, and mushrooms. Sauté for 12 minutes, until the veggies have softened, then add the garlic and ginger and sauté for another minute, until fragrant.

2. Add the water, tamari, corn, and soba noodles. Be sure to lay the noodles flat so they are completely covered with the water.

3. Set the trivet in the center of the pot. Place the tofu in a 6-inch round cake pan and cover with aluminum foil, then place the pan on the trivet.

4. Lock the lid into place. Select Pressure Cook and cook on high pressure for 4 minutes. When the cooking is complete, allow the pressure to release naturally for 10 minutes, then quick release any remaining pressure and remove the lid.

5. Divide the broth, noodles, and tofu evenly among four bowls and garnish with the scallions and avocado.

Flavor Boost: For some lemony tang, add some ground sumac or a squeeze of lemon juice.

PER SERVING (1 CUP): Calories 375, Total Fat 15g, Saturated Fat 2g, Cholesterol 0mg, Sodium 569mg, Potassium 776mg, Magnesium 132mg, Carbohydrates 47g, Sugars 5g, Added Sugars 0g, Fiber 6g, Protein 23g, Vitamin K 109mcg

CURRIED SOUP WITH CAULIFLOWER

DAIRY-FREE | GLUTEN-FREE | ONE-POT | QUICK

Canned pumpkin puree replaces the more often used coconut milk to keep this recipe lower in saturated fat. It also provides heart-healthy antioxidants, including beta-carotene.

Serves 4
Prep time: 5 minutes
Sauté: 4 minutes
Cook time: 4 minutes at high pressure
Pressure release: Natural for 10 minutes, then Quick
Total time: 28 minutes

3 teaspoons olive oil, divided

½ cup plus 2 tablespoons chopped scallions, divided

4 cups low-sodium chicken broth

1 pound cauliflower florets

1 (15-ounce) can pure pumpkin puree

1 tablespoon honey

¼ teaspoon salt

1½ tablespoons curry powder

3 garlic cloves, crushed

½ teaspoon ground cinnamon

¼ teaspoon ground cumin

1 cup dried red lentils

Freshly ground black pepper

Red pepper flakes (optional)

1. Select Sauté and wait 30 seconds for the Instant Pot to warm. Pour in 2 teaspoons of oil and heat for 30 seconds, until it starts to sizzle. Add ½ cup of scallions and sauté for about 3 minutes, until they start to brown.

2. Add the broth, cauliflower, pumpkin, honey, salt, curry powder, garlic, cinnamon, cumin, and lentils and stir.

3. Lock the lid into place. Select Pressure Cook and cook on high pressure for 4 minutes. When the cooking is complete, allow the pressure to release naturally for 10 minutes, then quick release any remaining pressure and remove the lid. The lentils should mush right into the mixture (the soup should be thick) and the cauliflower should be broken down and soft. Stir in the remaining 1 teaspoon of olive oil.

4. Divide among four bowls and garnish with the remaining 2 tablespoons of scallions, black pepper, and red pepper flakes, if desired.

PER SERVING (1 BOWL): Calories 334, Total Fat 7g, Saturated Fat 1g, Cholesterol 0mg, Sodium 264mg, Potassium 1,133mg, Magnesium 80mg, Carbohydrates 54g, Sugars 11g, Added Sugars 5g, Fiber 12g, Protein 20g, Vitamin K 42mcg

WHITE BEAN AND CORNMEAL CASSEROLE

DAIRY-FREE | GLUTEN-FREE | VEGETARIAN

This hearty casserole caters to many dietary needs, as it is vegetarian, gluten-free, and dairy-free. Plant-rich and whole food–based, it contains ample fiber and no added sugar.

Serves 6
Prep time: 10 minutes
Sauté: 7 minutes
Cook time: 10 minutes at high pressure
Pressure release: Natural for 5 minutes, then Quick
Total time: 37 minutes

1 cup cornmeal

1 cup unsweetened soy milk

1 tablespoon olive oil, divided

½ medium yellow onion, chopped

1 medium red or green bell pepper, chopped

1 teaspoon ground cumin

1 teaspoon crushed garlic

1½ cups water

Nonstick cooking spray

2 medium eggs, lightly beaten

1 (14.5-ounce) can low-sodium cannellini beans, drained and rinsed

1 cup frozen corn kernels

¼ teaspoon salt

1 (14.5-ounce) can no-salt-added diced tomatoes, drained, divided

1. In a medium bowl, soak the cornmeal in the soy milk for 7 to 10 minutes, until it resembles wet-packed sand.

2. Meanwhile, select Sauté and wait 30 seconds for the Instant Pot to warm. Pour in ½ tablespoon of oil and heat for 30 seconds, until it starts to sizzle. Add the onion and bell pepper and cook, stirring occasionally, for 5 minutes. Add the cumin and garlic and heat for another minute, until fragrant (add 1 tablespoon water if necessary to prevent sticking). Press Cancel and transfer the mixture to a bowl.

3. Pour 2 cups of water into the Instant Pot and set the trivet in the center. Fold an 18-inch sheet of aluminum foil lengthwise into thirds so it forms a 4-inch-wide strip. Place the foil strip over the trivet so the ends overhang the trivet evenly (this will make it easier to remove the cake pans from the Instant Pot after cooking). Coat two 6-inch round cake pans with nonstick spray.

PER SERVING: Calories 199, Total Fat 5g, Saturated Fat 1g, Cholesterol 55mg, Sodium 338mg, Potassium 528mg, Magnesium 42mg, Carbohydrates 31g, Sugars 7g, Added Sugars 0g, Fiber 7g, Protein 10g, Vitamin K 8mcg

4   Add the eggs, beans, corn, and salt to the cornmeal mixture and stir to combine, then gently fold in 1 cup of tomatoes, along with the sautéed bell peppers. Divide the mixture between the prepared cake pans. Cover both pans with aluminum foil. Stack them over the foil strip on the trivet and fold the ends of the strip over the pans so you'll be able to close the lid.

5   Lock the lid into place. Select Pressure Cook and cook on high pressure for 10 minutes. When the cooking is complete, allow the pressure to release naturally for 5 minutes, then quick release any remaining pressure and remove the lid.

6   Remove the pans and the foil. Garnish evenly with the remaining tomatoes. Run a knife between the pans and the casserole to loosen them, then cut each casserole into thirds and serve.

Variation Tip: Use 1 cup of chopped seeded shishito peppers in place of the bell pepper for a sweet and slightly smoky flavor.

LENTIL-WALNUT BOLOGNESE

DAIRY-FREE | VEGETARIAN | ONE-POT | WORTH THE WAIT

Veggie-rich tomato sauce is a great base for this dish, and once it's made, there are only a few more ingredients to add to the mix. Walnuts add a bit of crunch and heartiness to the pasta, while the lentils, rich in B vitamins and fiber, add creamy thickness like that of a traditional meat-based Bolognese.

Makes 4 cups
Prep time: 5 minutes
Cook time: 5 minutes at high pressure
Pressure release: Natural for 5 minutes, then Quick
Total time: 51 minutes (including time to make the sauce)

3 cups Zesty Carrot Tomato Sauce (page 119)

1 cup dried red lentils

¼ cup walnuts

4 ounces rotini pasta

1½ cups water

1 tablespoon low-sodium Worcestershire sauce

1 teaspoon low-sodium soy sauce

PER SERVING (1 CUP): Calories 395, Total Fat 9g, Saturated Fat 1g, Cholesterol 0mg, Sodium 375mg, Potassium 954mg, Magnesium 98mg, Carbohydrates 65g, Sugars 7g, Added Sugars 1g, Fiber 13g, Protein 19g, Vitamin K 15mcg

1 In the Instant Pot, combine the tomato sauce, lentils, walnuts, pasta, water, Worcestershire sauce, and soy sauce.

2 Lock the lid into place. Select Pressure Cook and cook on high pressure for 5 minutes. When the cooking is complete, allow the pressure to release naturally for 5 minutes, then quick release any remaining pressure and remove the lid.

3 Divide among four bowls and serve warm.

Substitution Tip: To make this vegan, swap out the Worcestershire sauce for additional low-sodium soy sauce, for a total of 1 tablespoon plus 1 teaspoon soy sauce.

STEAMED SALMON OVER HARVEST VEGGIES, PAGE 70

CHAPTER 5

SEAFOOD AND POULTRY

STEAMED TILAPIA WITH CREAMY BASIL SAUCE

QUICK

Mild tilapia gets a flavor boost from a creamy basil sauce, which keeps fat to a minimum thanks to gut-friendly Greek yogurt. The mix of zucchini and pasta makes this a well-balanced macro meal.

Serves 4
Prep time: 5 minutes
Cook time: 4 minutes at low pressure
Pressure release: Natural for 5 minutes, then Quick
Total time: 19 minutes

FOR THE SAUCE

1½ cups loosely packed fresh basil
1 cup plain low-fat Greek yogurt
Juice of 2 limes
¼ teaspoon salt
¼ cup olive oil
2 garlic cloves, crushed
1½ cups water

FOR THE FISH

4 ounces spaghetti or fettucine, broken in half
4 medium zucchini, sliced
1 pound tilapia
Freshly ground black pepper

TO MAKE THE SAUCE

1 In a blender, combine the basil, yogurt, lime juice, salt, oil, and garlic and blend for 30 seconds to 1 minute, until smooth and creamy. Set aside.

TO MAKE THE FISH

2 Pour 1½ cups of water into the Instant Pot, then add the pasta, ensuring that all the noodles are covered with water. Set the trivet on top.

3 Fold an 18-inch sheet of aluminum foil lengthwise into thirds so it forms a 4-inch-wide strip. Place the foil strip over the trivet so the ends overhang the trivet evenly (this will make it easier to remove the pan from the Instant Pot after cooking).

4 Place the zucchini and tilapia in a 6-inch round cake pan and cover with foil. Set the pan over the foil strip on the trivet and fold the ends of the strip over the pan so you'll be able to close the lid.

PER SERVING: Calories 359, Total Fat 13g, Saturated Fat 2.5g, Cholesterol 60mg, Sodium 286mg, Potassium 1,064mg, Magnesium 113mg, Carbohydrates 30g, Sugars 8g, Added Sugars 0g, Fiber 5g, Protein 34g, Vitamin K 44mcg

5   Lock the lid into place. Select Pressure Cook and cook on low pressure for 4 minutes. When the cooking is complete, allow the pressure to release naturally for 5 minutes, then quick release any remaining pressure and remove the lid. The fish should be moist and separate easily with a fork.

6   Carefully use the foil strip to lift out the pan with the veggies and fish. Drain any excess water from the pasta.

7   Portion out equal amounts of pasta, zucchini, and tilapia onto four plates. Drizzle 1 tablespoon of the sauce onto each. Season with pepper and serve.

STEAMED SALMON OVER HARVEST VEGGIES

GLUTEN-FREE | ONE-POT

Salmon is packed with anti-inflammatory omega-3s, healthy fats that support your brain and heart. According to the Mayo Clinic, these polyunsaturated fats lower triglycerides and may slightly reduce blood pressure.

Serves 4
Prep time: 10 minutes
Sauté: 9 minutes
Cook time: 4 minutes at high pressure
Pressure release: Natural for 5 minutes, then Quick
Total time: 33 minutes

1½ tablespoons olive oil, divided

2 cups coarsely chopped Brussels sprouts

1 cup water

1 medium red potato, chopped

1 cup cubed peeled sweet potato

4 (4-ounce) salmon fillets

¼ teaspoon salt, divided

2 teaspoons Italian seasoning

¾ teaspoon garlic powder, divided

2 cups baby spinach

¼ cup plain low-fat Greek yogurt

1 tablespoon fresh lemon juice

2 tablespoons water

1　Select Sauté and heat for 30 seconds until the Instant Pot is warmed. Pour in 1 tablespoon of oil and heat for 30 seconds, until it sizzles.

2　Add the Brussel sprouts to the pot and layer the potato and sweet potato on top. Sauté for 8 minutes, stirring once halfway through, until the Brussels sprouts have browned.

3　Pour 1 cup of water into the Instant Pot and set the trivet in the center.

4　Lay the salmon on one side of a 32-inch sheet of aluminum foil. Brush the remaining ½ tablespoon of oil over the salmon, then season with ⅛ teaspoon of salt, the Italian seasoning, and ½ teaspoon of garlic powder and top with the spinach. Fold the other side of the foil over the salmon and seal the edges tightly, then place the salmon on the trivet.

PER SERVING: Calories 367, Total Fat 11g, Saturated Fat 2g, Cholesterol 58mg, Sodium 275mg, Potassium 1,507mg, Magnesium 93mg, Carbohydrates 39g, Sugars 6g, Added Sugars 0g, Fiber 6g, Protein 29g, Vitamin K 90mcg

5 Lock the lid into place. Select Pressure Cook and cook on high pressure for 4 minutes. When the cooking is complete, allow the pressure to release naturally for 5 minutes, then quick release any remaining pressure and remove the lid. Transfer the fish to a plate. It should be moist and separate easily with a fork.

6 In a small bowl, whisk together the yogurt, lemon juice, remaining ⅛ teaspoon of salt, and remaining ¼ teaspoon of garlic powder. Add the water as needed until the sauce is thinned to your liking.

7 Portion out equal amounts of the veggies and salmon onto four plates. Drizzle with the yogurt sauce and serve.

Variation Tip: For extra heartiness, try adding a heart-healthy grain like farro.

LEMON AND DILL SALMON WITH POTATOES

DAIRY-FREE | GLUTEN-FREE | QUICK

The American Heart Association (AHA) recommends eating fish twice a week to reduce stroke risk. Eating more salmon is a great way to meet this recommendation. With dill, potatoes, peppers, and zucchini, this delicious meal is low in saturated fat and high in plant-based nutrients.

Serves 4
Prep time: 10 minutes
Cook time: 4 minutes at high pressure
Pressure release: Natural for 5 minutes, then Quick
Total time: 24 minutes

FOR THE DRESSING

2 tablespoons olive oil

Juice of 2 medium lemons

2 tablespoons chopped fresh dill

2 teaspoons honey

⅛ teaspoon salt

1½ cups water

FOR THE FISH AND POTATOES

8 small potatoes, sliced

1 large red bell pepper, chopped

2 medium zucchini, sliced

12 ounces salmon

1 tablespoon chopped fresh dill, for garnish

TO MAKE THE DRESSING

1 In a small bowl, whisk together the oil, lemon juice, dill, honey, and salt until well combined. Set aside.

TO MAKE THE FISH AND POTATOES

2 Pour 1½ cups of water into the Instant Pot, add the potatoes, and ensure they are all covered with water. Set the trivet on top.

3 Fold one 18-inch sheet of aluminum foil lengthwise into thirds so it forms a 4-inch-wide strip. Place one foil strip over the trivet so the ends overhang the trivet evenly (this will make it easier to remove the pan from the Instant Pot after cooking).

4 Place the bell pepper and zucchini in a 6-inch round cake pan and cover with foil. Set the pan over the foil strip on the trivet.

PER SERVING: Calories 454, Total Fat 11g, Saturated Fat 2g, Cholesterol 39mg, Sodium 167mg, Potassium 2,486mg, Magnesium 143mg, Carbohydrates 67g, Sugars 11g, Added Sugars 3g, Fiber 10g, Protein 24g, Vitamin K 13mcg

5   Place the salmon in the center of a large sheet of foil and drizzle half the dressing over the fish, then seal the foil tightly. Place the wrapped salmon on top of the cake pan, then fold the sides of the foil sling strip over the salmon so you'll be able to close the lid.

6   Lock the lid into place. Select Pressure Cook and cook on high pressure for 4 minutes. When the cooking is complete, allow the pressure to release naturally for 5 minutes, then quick release any remaining pressure and remove the lid. The fish should be moist and separate easily with a fork.

7   Using the foil strip, carefully lift out the salmon and vegetables. Drain any excess water from the potatoes and mix in the remaining dressing.

8   Portion out equal amounts of vegetables, potatoes, and fish onto four plates. Garnish with dill and serve.

Variation Tip: For a different veggie combo, you can swap out the bell pepper and zucchini for 2 cups of peas and carrots.

FISH TACOS WITH ZESTY LIME DRESSING

GLUTEN-FREE | ONE-POT | QUICK

Brightly flavored with a taco seasoning rub, simply steamed flaky cod fillets add heart-healthy antioxidants to these tacos.

Serves 4
Prep time: 10 minutes
Cook time: 3 minutes at high pressure
Pressure release: Natural for 2 minutes, then Quick
Total time: 20 minutes

FOR THE FISH

1 tablespoon olive oil

⅛ teaspoon salt

1 teaspoon ground cumin

1 teaspoon garlic powder

¼ teaspoon paprika

1 pound skinless cod, cut into 4 fillets

1½ cups water

FOR THE DRESSING

¼ cup plain low-fat Greek yogurt

Juice of 1 lime

1 teaspoon olive oil

1 tablespoon low-sodium ketchup

¼ teaspoon Dijon mustard

⅛ teaspoon salt

Pinch red pepper flakes or dash sriracha (optional)

FOR SERVING

4 corn tortillas

2 cups shredded red and green cabbage

1 medium avocado, chopped

TO MAKE THE FISH

1 In a small bowl, combine the olive oil, salt, cumin, garlic powder, and paprika. Rub it onto both sides of the cod fillets.

2 Pour 1½ cups of water into the Instant Pot and set the trivet in the center. Place a small square of aluminum foil on top of the trivet and place the cod fillets on the foil.

3 Lock the lid into place. Select Pressure Cook and cook on high pressure for 3 minutes. When the cooking is complete, allow the pressure to release naturally for 2 minutes, then quick release any remaining pressure and remove the lid. The fish should be moist and separate easily with a fork. Using tongs, carefully lift out the fish and transfer it to a plate.

TO MAKE THE DRESSING

4 In a small bowl, combine the yogurt, lime juice, oil, ketchup, mustard, salt, and red pepper flakes (if using).

TO SERVE

5 Place a fish fillet on each tortilla, flaking it with a fork if it is not already separated. Then distribute equal amounts of cabbage, avocado, and dressing onto each taco and serve.

PER SERVING (1 TACO): Calories 270, Total Fat 12g, Saturated Fat 2g, Cholesterol 60mg, Sodium 236mg, Potassium 723mg, Magnesium 65mg, Carbohydrates 19g, Sugars 3g, Added Sugars 1g, Fiber 5g, Protein 24g, Vitamin K 11mcg

FISH EN PAPILLOTE

DAIRY-FREE | ONE-POT | QUICK

With light, flaky tilapia and a colorful mélange of veggies, this one-pot fish dish is delightful to unwrap and full of heart-healthy nutrients. Tilapia is a delicate fish, so selecting a lower pressure setting helps ensure it doesn't get tough.

Serves 4
Prep time: 10 minutes
Cook time: 5 minutes at low pressure
Pressure release: Natural for 5 minutes, then Quick
Total time: 25 minutes

1½ cups water
4 (8-ounce) tilapia fillets, rinsed and patted dry, each cut in half
2 medium yellow squash, sliced
½ medium yellow onion, chopped
1 large red bell pepper, diced
4 scallions, green parts only, chopped
1 tablespoon olive oil
1 tablespoon fresh lemon juice
1 teaspoon herbes de Provence
½ teaspoon low-sodium soy sauce

PER SERVING: Calories 212, Total Fat 7g, Saturated Fat 2g, Cholesterol 65mg, Sodium 100mg, Potassium 819mg, Magnesium 65mg, Carbohydrates 8g, Sugars 5g, Added Sugars 0g, Fiber 2g, Protein 32g, Vitamin K 28mcg

1 Pour 1½ cups of water into the Instant Pot and set the trivet in the center.

2 Lay out four sheets of aluminum foil, about 16 inches long each. Layer the fish, squash, onion, bell pepper, and scallions in the center of each sheet of foil, dividing them evenly.

3 In a small bowl, mix the oil, lemon juice, herbes de Provence, and soy sauce. Pour an equal amount onto each portion of fish and vegetables. Wrap the fish and vegetables in the foil to make packets, sealing the edges tightly. Stack the foil packets on the trivet.

4 Lock the lid into place. Select Pressure Cook and cook on low pressure for 5 minutes. When the cooking is complete, allow the pressure to release naturally for 5 minutes, then quick release any remaining pressure. Remove the foil packets and carefully open one to check for doneness; the fish should be flaky and separate easily with a fork.

5 Place one foil packet onto each plate and unwrap when ready to eat.

Substitution Tip: To make this gluten-free, you can use ½ teaspoon of tamari (or ⅛ teaspoon of salt) instead of the soy sauce.

SHRIMP AND AVOCADO SALAD

DAIRY-FREE | GLUTEN-FREE | ONE-POT | QUICK

Avocados are packed with fiber! One medium avocado contains as much as 10 grams of fiber. Insoluble fiber supports digestion and soluble fiber aids in cholesterol control, and like many plant foods, avocados contain both. This salad pairs the superfood with heart-heathy, iron-rich shrimp and spinach.

Serves 4
Prep time: 5 minutes
Sauté: 7 minutes
Total time: 12 minutes

FOR THE DRESSING

Juice of 2 limes (about ¼ cup)

1 teaspoon honey

1 teaspoon olive oil

FOR THE SALAD

1 tablespoon olive oil

1½ pounds shrimp, peeled and deveined

4 cups baby spinach

2 medium radishes, thinly sliced

1 medium avocado, chopped

PER SERVING: Calories 271, Total Fat 12g, Saturated Fat 2g, Cholesterol 273mg, Sodium 231mg, Potassium 847mg, Magnesium 96mg, Carbohydrates 6g, Sugars 2g, Added Sugars 1g, Fiber 4g, Protein 36g, Vitamin K 157mcg

TO MAKE THE DRESSING

1 In a small bowl, whisk together the lime juice, honey, and olive oil. Set aside.

TO MAKE THE SALAD

2 Select Sauté and wait 30 seconds for the Instant Pot to warm. Pour in the oil and heat for 30 seconds, until it starts to sizzle. Add the shrimp and cook for 3 minutes on each side, until it turns pinkish-white throughout (you may want to cook it in two batches, using half the oil and half the shrimp for each). Transfer the shrimp to a plate.

3 Divide the spinach, radishes, avocado, shrimp, and dressing evenly among four bowls and serve.

Variation Tip: If you don't have limes, lemons will do. In fact, any citrus will add a refreshing tang. Just avoid grapefruit if you are on a statin medication.

LEMON-PEPPER SHRIMP OVER POLENTA

DAIRY-FREE | GLUTEN-FREE | 5 OR FEWER INGREDIENTS | ONE-POT QUICK

Shrimp contain magnesium, which helps regulate blood pressure by relaxing the blood vessels. Served up with fiber-rich asparagus, shrimp are ideal for both cholesterol and blood pressure control.

Serves 4
Prep time: 5 minutes
Sauté: 7 minutes
Steam: 10 minutes
Total time: 22 minutes

1 tablespoon olive oil

1½ pounds shrimp, peeled and deveined

⅛ teaspoon lemon-pepper seasoning

1½ cups water

1 cup polenta

1 pound asparagus, trimmed

3 tablespoons coarsely chopped fresh flat-leaf parsley

PER SERVING: Calories 327, Total Fat 5g, Saturated Fat 1g, Cholesterol 273mg, Sodium 215mg, Potassium 678mg, Magnesium 75mg, Carbohydrates 31g, Sugars 2g, Added Sugars 0g, Fiber 4g, Protein 40g, Vitamin K 49mcg

1. Select Sauté and wait 30 seconds for the Instant Pot to warm. Pour in the oil and heat for 30 seconds, until it starts to sizzle. Add the shrimp and cook for 3 minutes on each side, until it turns pinkish-white throughout (you may want to cook it in two batches, using half the oil and half the shrimp for each). Transfer the shrimp to a plate and season with the lemon-pepper seasoning.

2. Pour 1½ cups of water into the Instant Pot and set the trivet in the center. Wait about 5 minutes until the water starts to boil. Add the polenta and mix to ensure it is fully covered by the water.

3. Using tongs, carefully layer the asparagus on the trivet (or use a steamer basket that fits inside the Instant Pot).

4. Cover the pot with a clean kitchen towel and steam for 4 to 5 minutes, until the asparagus reaches the desired tenderness and the polenta is soft. Remove the towel and turn off the Instant Pot.

5. Portion the polenta onto four plates and place equal amounts of asparagus and shrimp on top. Garnish with the parsley and serve.

ORANGE CHICKEN WITH KALE AND CARROT SALAD

DAIRY-FREE | GLUTEN-FREE | ONE-POT | WORTH THE WAIT

Take-out orange chicken can contain as much as 1,700 milligrams of sodium per serving, and the added sugar is through the roof! This version is an equally tasty but much healthier option. Overall, each serving contains less than 400 milligrams of sodium and 8 grams of added sugar.

Serves 4
Prep time: 8 minutes
Sauté: 6 minutes
Cook time: 12 minutes at high pressure
Pressure release: Natural for 5 minutes, then Quick
Total time: 57 minutes (including time to make the sauce)

3 teaspoons olive oil, divided

½ medium yellow onion, chopped

1½ cups Sweet-and-Sour Orange Sauce (page 117)

⅓ cup low-sodium chicken broth

2 tablespoons low-sodium, low-sugar ketchup

4 (4-ounce) boneless, skinless chicken breasts, cut in half

6 cups chopped kale leaves

¼ teaspoon salt

¼ cup shredded carrot

¼ cup finely chopped fresh basil

1. Select Sauté and wait 30 seconds for the Instant Pot to warm. Pour in 2 teaspoons of oil and heat for 30 seconds, until it starts to sizzle. Add the onion and cook, stirring occasionally, for about 5 minutes, until it starts to soften.

2. Add the sweet-and-sour sauce, broth, ketchup, and chicken.

3. Lock the lid into place. Select Pressure Cook and cook on high pressure for 12 minutes. When the cooking is complete, allow the pressure to release naturally for 5 minutes, then quick release any remaining pressure and remove the lid. The chicken should be tender.

4. Meanwhile, in a medium bowl, with clean hands, massage the kale, salt, and remaining 1 teaspoon of olive oil for 3 to 5 minutes. Add the carrots.

5. Evenly divide the chicken pieces and sauce among four plates, top with fresh basil, and serve with equal portions of the kale and carrot salad.

Flavor Boost: Add a pinch or two of red pepper flakes for some heat.

PER SERVING: Calories 333, Total Fat 9g, Saturated Fat 2g, Cholesterol 96mg, Sodium 377mg, Potassium 657mg, Magnesium 56mg, Carbohydrates 25g, Sugars 16g, Added Sugars 8g, Fiber 3g, Protein 37g, Vitamin K 128mcg

CHICKEN MARGHERITA

ONE-POT | WORTH THE WAIT

Veggie-rich tomato sauce and leafy greens add antioxidant richness to this comforting chicken dish. By using skinless chicken breasts, you'll reduce saturated fat, while minimal amounts of oil and cheese further enhance the heart-healthy qualities of the dish.

Serves 4
Prep time: 5 minutes
Cook time: 12 minutes at high pressure
Pressure release: Natural for 5 minutes, then Quick
Total time: 58 minutes (including time to make the sauce)

FOR THE CHICKEN

1½ cups Zesty Carrot Tomato Sauce (page 119)

4 (4-ounce) boneless, skinless chicken breasts, sliced in half to form 8 (½-inch-thick) pieces

⅓ cup low-sodium chicken broth

FOR THE CHUNKY PESTO

½ cup chopped baby spinach

1 teaspoon crushed garlic

2 teaspoons olive oil

FOR SERVING

¼ cup grated Parmesan cheese

4 medium slices sourdough bread, toasted

TO MAKE THE CHICKEN

1 Pour the tomato sauce into the Instant Pot, then add the chicken and broth.

2 Lock the lid into place. Select Pressure Cook and cook on high pressure for 12 minutes. When the cooking is complete, allow the pressure to release naturally for 5 minutes, then quick release any remaining pressure and remove the lid. The chicken should be tender.

TO MAKE THE CHUNKY PESTO

3 In a small bowl, combine the spinach, garlic, and olive oil.

TO SERVE

4 Divide the chicken and sauce among four bowls. Evenly distribute the pesto and Parmesan on top of each and serve each with 1 slice of the toasted sourdough.

Variation Tip: If you prefer to serve this with rice instead of bread, add ⅔ cup of uncooked basmati rice and ⅔ cup of water in step 1.

PER SERVING: Calories 380, Total Fat 11g, Saturated Fat 3g, Cholesterol 107mg, Sodium 550mg, Potassium 626mg, Magnesium 57mg, Carbohydrates 24g, Sugars 4g, Added Sugars 0g, Fiber 3g, Protein 44g, Vitamin K 27mcg

BISCUIT-DUMPLING CHICKEN POTPIE

ONE-POT | WORTH THE WAIT

It's quite easy to prepare the biscuit dough for this recipe, and the dough contains no butter or lard, just a minimal amount of olive oil. One of the best things about potpie is that you can load it with a variety of veggies. All in all, you've got a heart-smart chicken potpie that's full of rich flavors while still keeping the saturated fat and sodium content in check.

Serves 6
Prep time: 10 minutes
Sauté: 14 minutes
Cook time: 12 minutes at high pressure
Pressure release: Natural for 5 minutes, then Quick
Total time: 46 minutes

FOR THE BISCUIT DUMPLING DOUGH

½ cup all-purpose flour
1 tablespoon olive oil
1 teaspoon baking soda
¼ cup low-fat milk

FOR THE FILLING

2 teaspoons olive oil
½ medium yellow onion, chopped
1 large red bell pepper, chopped
3 garlic cloves, minced
3 cups low-sodium chicken broth
1 cup water
2 cups chopped carrots

TO MAKE THE BISCUIT DUMPLING DOUGH

1 Pour the flour into a small bowl. Use a fork to mix in the oil until it forms loose crumbles, then stir in the baking soda and milk. The dough should be thick and pasty. Set aside.

TO MAKE THE FILLING

2 Select Sauté and wait 30 seconds for the Instant Pot to warm. Pour in the oil and heat for 30 seconds, until it sizzles. Add the onion and bell pepper and sauté, stirring occasionally, for 5 to 7 minutes, until the vegetables are soft (add 1 to 2 tablespoons water if necessary to preventing sticking), then stir in the garlic. Press Cancel.

3 Mix in the broth, water, carrots, broccoli, mushrooms, chicken, Italian seasoning, and Worcestershire. Select Sauté and bring the mixture to a boil, 3 to 5 minutes. Drop in the biscuit dough in rounded tablespoonfuls (you should have 6 dumplings) and simmer for 1 to 2 minutes, until the dumplings expand. Press Cancel.

2 cups small broccoli
  florets

1 cup chopped mushrooms

8 ounces boneless, skin-
  less chicken breast, cut
  into ½-inch cubes

1 tablespoon Italian
  seasoning

1 tablespoon low-sodium
  Worcestershire sauce

Freshly ground
  black pepper

PER SERVING (1 CUP FILLING AND
1 BISCUIT DUMPLING): Calories
330, Total Fat 10g, Saturated
Fat 2g, Cholesterol 49mg,
Sodium 506mg, Potassium
921mg, Magnesium 54mg,
Carbohydrates 35g, Sugars
9g, Added Sugars 1g, Fiber 6g,
Protein 27g, Vitamin K 68mcg

4 Lock the lid into place. Select Pressure Cook and
   cook on high pressure for 12 minutes. When the
   cooking is complete, allow the pressure to release
   naturally for 5 minutes, then quick release any
   remaining pressure and remove the lid. The
   chicken should be tender.

5 Use a slotted spoon to transfer the biscuit dumplings to a plate.

6 Divide the chicken filling among six bowls and
   add 1 biscuit dumpling to each. Season with
   pepper and serve.

Substitution Tip: If you prefer a vegetarian version, you
can omit the chicken breast and prepare Simple Veggie
Broth (page 126) and use instead of the chicken broth.

CHICKEN SATAY WITH GREEN BEANS

DAIRY-FREE | QUICK

A sweet and savory sauce is a lovely thing, made even better when it's a source of heart-healthy fats and low in added sugars.

Serves 4
Prep time: 5 minutes
Cook time: 12 minutes at high pressure
Pressure release: Natural for 3 minutes, then Quick
Total time: 25 minutes

FOR THE SATAY SAUCE

3 tablespoons no-sugar-added natural peanut butter

1 tablespoon low-sodium soy sauce

3 garlic cloves, minced

1 teaspoon finely grated fresh ginger

2 teaspoons honey

2 teaspoons plus 1½ cups water

TO MAKE THE SATAY SAUCE

1 In a small bowl, whisk together the peanut butter, soy sauce, garlic, ginger, and honey until well combined. Add 1 to 2 teaspoons water as needed to create a thick but pourable consistency. Set aside.

TO MAKE THE CHICKEN AND RICE

2 Pour 1½ cups of water into the Instant Pot and add the rice. Set the trivet in the center.

3 Place the chicken cubes in a 6-inch round cake pan and fully coat with the satay sauce. Cover with aluminum foil and place the pan on the trivet.

4 Place the frozen green beans in another 6-inch round cake pan and mix in the soy sauce and garlic powder. Cover tightly with foil and stack on top of the other cake pan.

FOR THE CHICKEN AND RICE

¾ cup uncooked
  brown rice

12 ounces boneless, skin-
  less chicken breasts, cut
  into 1-inch cubes

1 pound frozen cut
  green beans

1 teaspoon low-sodium
  soy sauce

¼ teaspoon garlic powder

PER SERVING: Calories 368, Total Fat 10g, Saturated Fat 2g, Cholesterol 60mg, Sodium 285mg, Potassium 600mg, Magnesium 65mg, Carbohydrates 40g, Sugars 6g, Added Sugars 3g, Fiber 5g, Protein 29g, Vitamin K 1mcg

5 Lock the lid into place. Select Pressure Cook and cook on high pressure for 12 minutes. When the cooking is complete, allow the pressure to release naturally for 3 minutes, then quick release any remaining pressure and remove the lid.

6 Carefully remove the cake pans, remove the foil, and let cool for a few minutes. Gently remove the trivet and drain any excess water from the rice.

7 Divide the seasoned green beans evenly among four bowls, then top evenly with the chicken and rice. Pour any remaining satay sauce over the rice for more flavor and serve.

CHICKEN AND MUSHROOM RISOTTO

ONE-POT | WORTH THE WAIT

Using homemade cream of mushroom soup keeps this dish well within heart-healthy sodium limits and adds an earthy flavor. This satisfying risotto also packs in 22 grams of protein.

Serves 4
Prep time: 5 minutes
Cook time: 12 minutes at high pressure
Pressure release: Natural for 5 minutes, then Quick
Total time: 58 minutes (including time to make the soup)

2 cups Cream of Mushroom Soup (page 125)

6 ounces boneless, skinless chicken breast, cut into ½-inch cubes

¾ cup uncooked arborio rice

½ cup water

3 garlic cloves, crushed

¼ teaspoon salt

⅛ teaspoon ground cumin

¼ cup grated Parmesan cheese

⅛ teaspoon sweet paprika

PER SERVING: Calories 304, Total Fat 8g, Saturated Fat 2g, Cholesterol 45mg, Sodium 400mg, Potassium 22mg, Magnesium 30mg, Carbohydrates 35g, Sugars 5g, Added Sugars 0g, Fiber 2g, Protein 22g, Vitamin K 4mcg

1 Pour the mushroom soup into the Instant Pot, then add the chicken, rice, water, and garlic. Stir well.

2 Lock the lid into place. Select Pressure Cook and cook on high pressure for 12 minutes. When the cooking is complete, allow the pressure to release naturally for 5 minutes, then quick release any remaining pressure and remove the lid. The chicken should be tender and the rice should be soft and creamy.

3 Mix in the salt and cumin. Garnish with the Parmesan and paprika and serve.

Flavor Boost: To brighten the overall flavor of this dish, garnish with 1 tablespoon of chopped fresh flat-leaf parsley.

CHILI CON CARNE, PAGE 97

BEEF AND PORK

BRISKET AND KASHA STEW

DAIRY-FREE | ONE-POT | WORTH THE WAIT

This simple stew takes little time—the Instant Pot does all the work to tenderize the meat and bring out good flavor. Much of the flavoring comes from the home-made BBQ sauce, but there are definitely some veggie flavor additions that make this meal unique. Carrots and bell peppers also deliver the antioxidant beta-carotene, which, when consumed as part of a plant-rich diet, may help protect against atherosclerosis, according to the Cleveland Clinic.

Serves 4
Prep time: 5 minutes
Cook time: 1 hour at high pressure
Pressure release: Natural for 25 minutes, then Quick
Total time: 1 hour 43 minutes (including time to make the sauce)

1 cup Sweet-and-Tangy BBQ Sauce (page 116)

¾ cup low-sodium chicken broth

1¾ cups water

1 tablespoon low-sodium soy sauce

1 tablespoon garlic powder

3 cups chopped carrots

2 large red bell peppers, sliced

12 ounces lean stew beef

1 cup kasha (buckwheat groats)

PER SERVING: Calories 367, Total Fat 6g, Saturated Fat 2g, Cholesterol 53mg, Sodium 511mg, Potassium 752mg, Magnesium 121mg, Carbohydrates 56g, Sugars 16g, Added Sugars 6g, Fiber 9g, Protein 26g, Vitamin K 14mcg

1. Pour the BBQ sauce into the Instant Pot and add the broth, water, soy sauce, garlic powder, carrots, peppers, beef, and kasha. Stir until well combined.

2. Lock the lid into place. Select Pressure Cook and cook on high pressure for 1 hour. When the cooking is complete, allow the pressure to release naturally for 25 minutes, then quick release any remaining pressure and remove the lid.

3. Divide among four bowls and serve warm.

Flavor Boost: To spice things up, add a little sriracha to each bowl of stew.

PULLED PORK STEW

DAIRY-FREE | ONE-POT | WORTH THE WAIT

This stew has a wonderful barbecue appeal thanks to its crave-worthy sauce and thick texture. Making the stew with homemade BBQ sauce means you get all the good, zesty flavor of traditional barbecue without excess sugar and sodium.

Serves 4
Prep time: 5 minutes
Sauté: 5 minutes
Cook time: 1 hour at high pressure
Pressure release: Natural for 25 minutes, then Quick
Total time: 1 hour 48 minutes (including time to make the sauce)

1 tablespoon olive oil

8 ounces round-cut pork (two 1½-inch-thick fillets), cut into 2-inch-thick strips

1 cup Sweet-and-Tangy BBQ Sauce (page 116)

¾ cup low-sodium chicken broth

1 tablespoon low-sodium soy sauce

¾ cup water

1 cup baby spinach

2 large red bell peppers, sliced

PER SERVING: Calories 173, Total Fat 7g, Saturated Fat 1g, Cholesterol 37mg, Sodium 427mg, Potassium 612mg, Magnesium 39mg, Carbohydrates 15g, Sugars 11g, Added Sugars 6g, Fiber 3g, Protein 15g, Vitamin K 42mcg

1   Select Sauté and wait 30 seconds for the Instant Pot to warm. Pour in the oil and heat for 30 seconds, until it starts to sizzle. Add the pork and sear it for 3 to 4 minutes on each side, until the outside is browned but the inner meat is still pink.

2   Add the BBQ sauce, broth, soy sauce, water, spinach, and bell peppers. Stir well to combine.

3   Lock the lid into place. Select Pressure Cook and cook on high pressure for 1 hour. When the cooking is complete, allow the pressure to release naturally for 25 minutes, then quick release any remaining pressure and remove the lid.

4   Divide among four bowls and serve warm.

Variation Tip: To change it up a bit, swap out the bell peppers for 1 cup of chopped carrots and 1 medium potato (diced), then add ½ teaspoon of ground cumin.

GARLIC-BALSAMIC BEEF SKEWERS

DAIRY-FREE | GLUTEN-FREE | WORTH THE WAIT

Filled with bell peppers, mushrooms, and zucchini, this dish supplies a diversity of vitamins and minerals. The American Heart Association (AHA) recommends an emphasis on plant foods in the diet to help lower the risk of heart attack and stroke.

Serves 3
Prep time: 8 minutes, plus 1 hour to marinate
Sauté: 5 minutes
Cook time: 2 minutes at high pressure
Pressure release: Natural for 5 minutes, then Quick
Total time: 1 hour 25 minutes

FOR THE MARINADE

½ cup aged balsamic vinegar
2 tablespoons low-sodium Worcestershire sauce
1 teaspoon garlic powder
1 pound sirloin steak, cut into 1-inch cubes

FOR THE SKEWERS

1 tablespoon olive oil
1 cup low-sodium chicken broth
2 large red bell peppers, chopped into 1-inch pieces
2 cups sliced mushrooms
1 medium zucchini, sliced
½ teaspoon garlic powder

TO MAKE THE MARINADE

1 In a medium bowl, combine the vinegar, Worcestershire, and garlic powder, then portion out half into an airtight container; set the remainder aside. Add the steak cubes to the container, mix well, cover, and marinate for 1 hour.

TO MAKE THE SKEWERS

2 Select Sauté and wait 30 seconds for the Instant Pot to warm. Pour in the oil and heat for 30 seconds, until it starts to sizzle. Add the steak cubes with the marinade, then cook for 3 minutes. Gently flip to another side and sauté for 1 minute more (it's okay if there's still some pink color to the meat).

3 Add the broth to the pot so that it covers the meat by three-quarters. Place the trivet on top. Place the peppers, mushrooms, and zucchini in a 6-inch round cake pan and set it on top of the trivet.

PER SERVING (2 SKEWERS): Calories 355, Total Fat 8g, Saturated Fat 3g, Cholesterol 92mg, Sodium 174mg, Potassium 1,327mg, Magnesium 75mg, Carbohydrates 29g, Sugars 23g, Added Sugars 1g, Fiber 4g, Protein 39g, Vitamin K 12mcg

4 Lock the lid into place. Select Pressure Cook and cook on high pressure for 2 minutes. When the cooking is complete, allow the pressure to release naturally for 5 minutes, then quick release any remaining pressure and remove the lid.

5 Remove all the ingredients from the Instant Pot. Skewer the veggies and beef, alternating between them, and transfer to a large plate.

6 Drizzle the reserved marinade over the skewers and dust with garlic powder. Serve immediately.

Ingredient Tip: Do not use tough cuts such as stew beef, as the meat will come out tough in this shorter process. Tender cuts such as sirloin work well to ensure a tender result, especially after marinating. Aged balsamic is a sweeter and thicker vinegar, but you can also use non-aged.

ZESTY MEAT LOAF

DAIRY-FREE | ONE-POT | WORTH THE WAIT

Convenient and delicious, this meat loaf is made with simple ingredients, including frozen peas and carrots you may already have in your freezer. Easy recipes help keep you on track for heart-healthy eating because you don't have to fuss over ingredients or complicated directions. Although ketchup is pretty standard for most meat loaves, the sweet-and-tangy BBQ sauce adds a unique flavor to this tasty, veggie-rich loaf.

Serves 4
Prep time: 10 minutes
Cook time: 30 minutes at high pressure
Pressure release: Natural for 10 minutes, then Quick
Total time: 1 hour 5 minutes (including time to make the sauce, plus resting time)

1 pound 85% lean ground beef

1 medium egg

1 cup panko bread crumbs

1 cup frozen peas and carrots

1½ cups Sweet-and-Tangy BBQ Sauce (page 116), divided

1 cup water

4 medium sweet potatoes, cut into ½-inch-thick rounds

8 cups baby spinach

1. In a large bowl, combine the ground beef, egg, bread crumbs, peas and carrots, and ½ cup of BBQ sauce. Use clean hands to mix until well incorporated.

2. Form the mixture into an 8-inch-long loaf on a large sheet of aluminum foil, then wrap it in the foil, exposing only the top of the loaf.

3. Pour 1 cup of water into the Instant Pot. Add the sweet potato rounds. Top with the trivet and place the foil-wrapped meat loaf on the trivet.

4. Lock the lid into place. Select Pressure Cook and cook on high pressure for 30 minutes. When the cooking is complete, allow the pressure to release naturally for 10 minutes, then quick release any remaining pressure and remove the lid. Turn off the Instant Pot. Remove the lid and unwrap the meat loaf so the top is exposed.

PER SERVING: Calories 295, Total Fat 9g, Saturated Fat 3, Cholesterol 70mg, Sodium 325mg, Potassium 727mg, Magnesium 54mg, Carbohydrates 34g, Sugars 10g, Added Sugars 3g, Fiber 4g, Protein 19g, Vitamin K 148mcg

5   Pour the remaining 1 cup of BBQ sauce on the top of the meat loaf, cover the Instant Pot with a clean kitchen towel, and let it rest for 10 minutes, until the sauce is warmed.

6   Carefully transfer the meat loaf to a cutting board and slice into eight ½-inch-thick slices. Transfer the sweet potatoes to a plate.

7   Divide the baby spinach among four plates and top each with 1 slice of the meat loaf, then drizzle with the sauce. Place 3 or 4 sweet potato slices alongside and serve. Transfer the remaining 4 slices of meat loaf to an airtight container and store in the refrigerator for up to 4 days.

EGG ROLL IN A BOWL

DAIRY-FREE | QUICK

Traditional deep-fried egg rolls aren't part of a heart-healthy diet, but this Instant Pot version lets you enjoy their rich flavors without the saturated fat. With fresh ginger, garlic, and ground pork, the aromas in this dish are incredible.

Serves 4
Prep time: 5 minutes
Sauté: 7 minutes
Pressure release: Quick
Total time: 17 minutes

2 tablespoons toasted sesame oil, divided

½ medium Vidalia onion, chopped

2 teaspoons finely grated fresh ginger

2 garlic cloves, crushed

4 ounces 80% lean ground pork

1 cup frozen peas

2 medium egg whites

2 tablespoons low-sodium soy sauce

2 tablespoons unseasoned rice vinegar

4 cups shredded cabbage or mixed shredded cabbage and carrot

½ cup water

Sliced scallions, for garnish

PER SERVING: Calories 225, Total Fat 13g, Saturated Fat 3g, Cholesterol 20mg, Sodium 380mg, Potassium 405mg, Magnesium 26mg, Carbohydrates 17g, Sugars 8g, Added Sugars 0g, Fiber 4g, Protein 11g, Vitamin K 14mcg

1 Select Sauté and wait 30 seconds for the Instant Pot to warm. Pour in 1 teaspoon of sesame oil and heat for 30 seconds, until it starts to sizzle. Add the onion, ginger, garlic, and ground pork. Break up the pork with a spatula and cook, stirring occasionally, for 3 to 4 minutes, until the pork is nearly browned throughout.

2 Add the peas and egg whites to the pork mixture and cook, stirring, for 2 minutes more, until the egg whites are solid.

3 Mix in the remaining sesame oil, soy sauce, and vinegar. Add the cabbage and water. Press Cancel.

4 Lock the lid into place. Select Pressure Cook and cook on high pressure for 0 minutes. Pressure will build for 6 minutes to steam the cabbage. Quick release the pressure and remove the lid.

5 Divide the cabbage mixture among four bowls. Top each with about ½ cup of the pork mixture. Garnish with scallions and serve.

BEEF STROGANOFF

ONE-POT | WORTH THE WAIT

This recipe calls for considerably less beef than traditional stroganoff. It also has far less sodium, and using 85 percent lean meat keeps the saturated fat low.

Serves 4
Prep time: 5 minutes
Sauté: 6 minutes
Cook time: 2 minutes at high pressure
Pressure release: Natural for 12 minutes, then Quick
Total time: 45 minutes (including time to make the soup, plus cooling time)

Nonstick cooking spray

4 ounces 85% lean ground beef

¼ teaspoon garlic powder

1 tablespoon white wine vinegar or white balsamic vinegar

2 cups Cream of Mushroom Soup (page 125)

1 cup water

4 ounces pasta (see Ingredient Tip)

1 teaspoon Italian seasoning

¼ cup plain low-fat Greek yogurt

¼ teaspoon salt

Freshly ground black pepper (optional)

1 Select Sauté and wait 30 seconds for the Instant Pot to warm. Coat the inner pot lightly with nonstick spray and heat for 30 seconds. Add the beef and garlic powder. Use a spatula to break up the beef and cook for 5 minutes, until it is mostly browned. Add the vinegar and scrape up any browned bits from the pot with the spatula.

2 Add the cream of mushroom soup, water, pasta, and Italian seasoning and stir.

3 Lock the lid into place. Select Pressure Cook and cook on high pressure for 2 minutes. When the cooking is complete, allow the pressure to release naturally for 12 minutes, then quick release any remaining pressure and remove the lid.

4 Remove the mixture from the pot and let cool for about 15 minutes, then mix in the yogurt, salt, and pepper to taste, if desired, and serve.

Ingredient Tip: Spiral rotini noodles hold sauce well, but you can also use fettucine or a thick, wide noodle instead.

PER SERVING: Calories 311, Total Fat 12g, Saturated Fat 3g, Cholesterol 28mg, Sodium 259mg, Potassium 457mg, Magnesium 24mg, Carbohydrates 24g, Sugars 7g, Added Sugars 0g, Fiber 13g, Protein 29g, Vitamin K 7mcg

RIGATONI WITH MEAT SAUCE

DAIRY-FREE | ONE-POT

With a variety of veggies, this sauce offers a good dose of potassium to keep blood pressure in check, plus a natural boost of fiber for cholesterol control. There's just enough meat in the sauce to provide a delectable, rich flavor, too.

Serves 4
Prep time: 10 minutes
Sauté: 6 minutes
Cook time: 3 minutes at high pressure
Pressure release: Natural for 12 minutes, then Quick
Total time: 36 minutes

Nonstick cooking spray

6 ounces 85% lean ground beef

1 cup chopped yellow onion

6 ounces rigatoni pasta

1½ cups chopped zucchini

1½ cups chopped red bell pepper

1 cup shredded carrots

2½ cups low-sodium marinara sauce, divided

2½ cups water

1 teaspoon garlic powder

1 teaspoon Italian seasoning or poultry seasoning

PER SERVING: Calories 384, Total Fat 12g, Saturated Fat 3g, Cholesterol 37mg, Sodium 236mg, Potassium 1,068mg, Magnesium 81mg, Carbohydrates 52g, Sugars 12g, Added Sugars 0g, Fiber 9g, Protein 20g, Vitamin K 10mcg

1 Select Sauté and wait 30 seconds for the Instant Pot to warm. Lightly coat the inner pot with nonstick spray and heat for 30 seconds. Add the beef and onion. Use a spatula to break up the beef and cook for 5 minutes, until it is mostly browned. Press Cancel.

2 Add the pasta, zucchini, bell peppers, carrots, 1½ cups of marinara, and the water. (The pasta needs to remain completely submerged in liquid, so add more water and marinara if needed to cover.)

3 Lock the lid into place. Select Pressure Cook and cook on high pressure for 3 minutes. When the cooking is complete, allow the pressure to release naturally for 12 minutes, then quick release any remaining pressure and remove the lid.

4 Mix in the remaining 1 cup of marinara to thicken, along with the garlic powder and the Italian seasoning or poultry seasoning, and serve.

Ingredient Tip: Choose a low-sodium marinara with 200 milligrams (or less) sodium per serving.

CHILI CON CARNE

DAIRY-FREE | ONE-POT

Sautéing sears in flavor. The low-sodium beans and tomatoes are punched up with cumin, garlic, and paprika.

Serves 4
Prep time: 10 minutes
Sauté: 6 minutes
Cook time: 5 minutes at high pressure
Pressure release: Natural for 10 minutes, then Quick
Total time: 36 minutes

Nonstick cooking spray

6 ounces 85% lean ground beef

1 medium yellow onion, diced

3 green bell peppers, diced

2 shishito peppers, seeded and finely sliced

1 (14-ounce) can low-sodium diced tomatoes

1 cup low-sodium marinara sauce

½ cup low-sodium chicken broth

1 tablespoon low-sodium soy sauce

1 teaspoon garlic powder

¾ teaspoon ground cumin

¼ teaspoon smoked paprika

1 (14-ounce) can low-sodium kidney beans or cannellini beans drained and rinsed

1   Select Sauté and wait 30 seconds for the Instant Pot to warm. Coat the inner pot lightly with non-stick spray and heat for 30 seconds. Add the beef and onion. Break up the meat with a spatula and cook for 3 minutes, until the beef is only slightly pink. Add the bell peppers and shishito peppers. Sauté for 2 to 3 minutes more. Press Cancel.

2   Add the diced tomatoes with their juices, marinara, broth, soy sauce, garlic powder, cumin, paprika, and beans. Stir well to combine.

3   Lock the lid into place. Select Pressure Cook and cook on high pressure for 5 minutes. When the cooking is complete, allow the pressure to release naturally for 10 minutes, then quick release any remaining pressure and remove the lid.

4   Serve warm.

Flavor Boost: If you like, add ½ cup of Sweet-and-Tangy BBQ Sauce (page 116) to the other ingredients in step 2.

PER SERVING: Calories 371, Total Fat 9g, Saturated Fat 3g, Cholesterol 33mg, Sodium 325mg, Potassium 881mg, Magnesium 66mg, Carbohydrates 48g, Sugars 16g, Added Sugars 2g, Fiber 12g, Protein 25g, Vitamin K 18mcg

PORK AND ASPARAGUS WRAPS

DAIRY-FREE | GLUTEN-FREE | ONE-POT | QUICK

These delicious lettuce wraps have a small but intensely flavorful amount of lean ground pork, making them low in saturated fat.

Serves 4
Prep time: 5 minutes
Steam: 10 minutes
Sauté: 7 minutes
Total time: 22 minutes

1½ cups water

16 medium asparagus
   spears, trimmed

Nonstick cooking spray

4 ounces 80% lean
   ground pork

½ medium yellow
   onion, diced

2 teaspoons ground cumin

2 teaspoons garlic powder

1 teaspoon smoked paprika

¼ teaspoon salt

8 large crisp romaine lettuce leaves

8 ounces firm tofu, cubed

PER SERVING (1 LETTUCE WRAP):
Calories 161, Total Fat 9g,
Saturated Fat 3g, Cholesterol
20mg, Sodium 182mg,
Potassium 367mg, Magnesium
47mg, Carbohydrates 9g, Sugars
3g, Added Sugars 0g, Fiber 3g,
Protein 14g, Vitamin K 57mcg

1   Pour 1½ cups of water into the Instant Pot and set the trivet in the center. Select Sauté and bring the water to a boil, about 5 minutes.

2   Using tongs, carefully layer the asparagus over the trivet, arranging the top layer of asparagus perpendicular to the bottom layer.

3   Cover the Instant Pot with a clean kitchen towel and steam the asparagus for 4 to 5 minutes, until it reaches your desired tenderness.

4   Press Cancel. Transfer the asparagus to a plate. Chop it into small pieces and set aside.

5   Dump out the water, wipe the inner liner dry, and return it to the Instant Pot.

6   Select Sauté and wait 30 seconds for the Instant Pot to warm. Lightly coat the inner pot with nonstick spray and heat for 30 seconds. Add the ground pork and onion and sauté for 5 minutes, using a spatula to break up the meat, until the pork is browned and no longer pink. Mix in the cumin, garlic powder, paprika, and salt and continue to heat for 1 more minute. Transfer the pork mixture to a bowl.

7   Fill each romaine leaf with equal amounts of seasoned pork, tofu, and asparagus.

RED CURRY BEEF BOWLS

This filling Thai-inspired dish has less saturated fat than traditional red curry because it doesn't use heavy coconut milk. The carrots add sweetness while the combo of spices and fish sauce keep it tangy and aromatic. Without excess salt or sugars, this is a terrific, flavorful, heart-healthy option.

Serves 4
Prep time: 5 minutes
Sauté: 5 minutes
Cook time: 5 minutes at high pressure
Pressure release: Natural for 10 minutes, then Quick
Total time: 30 minutes

Nonstick cooking spray

6 ounces beef tenderloin or sirloin, cut into thin strips

1 medium yellow onion, diced

1 medium green bell pepper, diced

2 shishito peppers, seeded and finely sliced

1 cup shredded carrots

½ cup low-sodium marinara sauce

1½ tablespoons fish sauce

1 tablespoon crushed garlic

1 teaspoon grated fresh ginger

1 tablespoon ground cumin

1 tablespoon ground coriander

¾ cup uncooked brown rice

1½ cups water

1   Select Sauté and wait 30 seconds for the Instant Pot to warm. Lightly coat the inner pot with nonstick spray and heat for 30 seconds. Insert the beef and onion and cook, stirring occasionally, for 3 minutes, until the beef is nearly browned. Add the bell and shishito peppers. Sauté for 2 to 3 minutes more.

2   Add the carrots, marinara, fish sauce, garlic, ginger, cumin, coriander, brown rice, and water (make sure the water covers the rice and add more if needed).

3   Lock the lid into place. Select Pressure Cook and cook on high pressure for 5 minutes. When the cooking is complete, allow the pressure to release naturally for 10 minutes, then quick release any remaining pressure and remove the lid.

4   Stir well and divide among four bowls.

PER SERVING: Calories 243, Total Fat 5g, Saturated Fat 1g, Cholesterol 33mg, Sodium 556mg, Potassium 486mg, Magnesium 34mg, Carbohydrates 32g, Sugars 6g, Added Sugars 0g, Fiber 4g, Protein 20g, Vitamin K 5mcg

HARVEST FRUIT CRISP, PAGE 105

CHAPTER 7

SNACKS AND TREATS

ROSEMARY-GARLIC CASHEWS

**DAIRY-FREE | VEGETARIAN | 5 OR FEWER INGREDIENTS
ONE-POT | QUICK**

*Toasty and bursting with flavor, this recipe makes a delightful crunchy snack,
perfect to share with guests. Cashews are heart-healthy because they are
nutrient-dense and a good source of healthy fats. While it may sound easier to
toss everything in the pot and sauté it all together, you'll have best results (and
less sticky residue in the pot) if you season with half the spices while cooking, and
the remaining ingredients right after cooking when the cashews are still warm.*

Serves 8
Prep time: 5 minutes
Sauté: 5 minutes
Total time: 10 minutes

1 tablespoon olive oil

2 cups whole cashews

1 tablespoon low-sodium
soy sauce

1 teaspoon garlic
powder, divided

1 tablespoon chopped fresh
rosemary, divided

2 teaspoons honey

PER SERVING (3 TABLESPOONS):
Calories 157, Total Fat 12g,
Saturated Fat 2g, Cholesterol
0mg, Sodium 75mg, Potassium
171mg, Magnesium 73mg,
Carbohydrates 9g, Sugars
3g, Added Sugars 1g, Fiber 1g,
Protein 5g, Vitamin K 9mcg

1 Select Sauté and wait 30 seconds for the
Instant Pot to warm. Pour in the oil and heat
for 30 seconds, until it starts to sizzle. Add the
cashews, soy sauce, ½ teaspoon of garlic powder,
and 2 teaspoons of rosemary. Cook, stirring,
for 3 to 5 minutes, or until the cashews start to
brown and their aroma releases.

2 Press Cancel. Mix in the remaining ½ teaspoon of
garlic powder, the remaining 1 teaspoon of rosemary, and the honey. Transfer to a parchment
paper–lined baking sheet in an even layer, and let
cool for 3 minutes before enjoying.

Variation Tip: For a spicy mixed-nut blend, swap out
half the cashews for walnuts and add a pinch of red
pepper flakes.

GARLIC EDAMAME

DAIRY-FREE | VEGAN | 5 OR FEWER INGREDIENTS | ONE-POT | QUICK

Edamame is sautéed to perfection with low-sodium soy sauce and crisp, golden garlic for a rich, aromatic flavor. Edamame is a good source of plant protein and also provides soluble fiber and vitamin K—both of which help maintain desirable cholesterol levels for reduced risk of heart disease.

Serves 4
Prep time: 5 minutes
Sauté: 5 minutes
Total time: 10 minutes

1 tablespoon olive oil
2 garlic cloves, thinly sliced
2 teaspoons low-sodium soy sauce
1 cup fresh or frozen shelled edamame

PER SERVING (¼ CUP): Calories 81, Total Fat 5g, Saturated Fat 1g, Cholesterol 0mg, Sodium 98mg, Potassium 184mg, Magnesium 27mg, Carbohydrates 4g, Sugars 1g, Added Sugars 0g, Fiber 2g, Protein 5g, Vitamin K 12mcg

1   Select Sauté and wait 30 seconds for the Instant Pot to warm. Pour in the oil and heat for 30 seconds, until it starts to sizzle.

2   Add the garlic and stir for 1 to 2 minutes, until it is crisp and golden. Transfer it to a medium bowl and set aside.

3   Pour the soy sauce and edamame into the Instant Pot. Toss well to coat and sauté for 1 to 3 minutes, until the edamame is warmed. Press Cancel.

4   Transfer the edamame to the bowl with the garlic and mix well before serving.

Ingredient Tip: If you don't have fresh garlic, season the edamame with ½ teaspoon of garlic powder once they are warmed.

BLACK BEAN BROWNIE BITES

VEGETARIAN | WORTH THE WAIT

You won't taste the beans in these deliciously dense brownies, but you will get plenty of heart-healthy fiber from them. Beans also provide B vitamins, including folate, which helps protect the lining of your blood vessels.

Makes 7 brownie bites
Prep time: 5 minutes
Cook time: 20 minutes at high pressure
Pressure release: Natural for 12 minutes, then Quick
Total time: 52 minutes (including time to make the sweet bean filling, plus cooling time)

1½ cups water

Nonstick cooking spray

¾ batch Sweet Bean Filling (page 45)

¼ cup packed brown sugar

2½ tablespoons avocado oil

1 tablespoon cashew butter

1 medium egg

½ teaspoon vanilla extract

1 tablespoon unsweetened cocoa powder

¼ cup all-purpose flour

½ teaspoon baking soda

28 dark chocolate chips (at least 70% cacao)

PER SERVING (1 BROWNIE BITE):
Calories 200, Total Fat 10g, Saturated Fat 2g, Cholesterol 27mg, Sodium 101mg, Potassium 216mg, Magnesium 32mg, Carbohydrates 25g, Sugars 12g, Added Sugars 6g, Fiber 4g, Protein 4g, Vitamin K 8mcg

1 Pour 1½ cups of water into the Instant Pot and set the trivet in the center. Coat a 7-cup silicone egg mold with nonstick spray.

2 In a medium bowl, combine the bean filling, brown sugar, oil, cashew butter, egg, and vanilla and mix until well combined.

3 Mix in the cocoa powder, flour, and baking soda. Divide the batter evenly among the wells of the prepared egg mold. Add 4 chocolate chips to the tops of each. Cover the mold with its lid or aluminum foil. Place the egg mold on the trivet.

4 Lock the lid into place. Select Pressure Cook and cook on high pressure for 20 minutes. When the cooking is complete, allow the pressure to release naturally for 12 minutes, then quick release any remaining pressure and remove the lid.

5 Remove the mold and uncover it. Let the brownie bites cool for at least 10 minutes before carefully removing them from the mold and serving.

Ingredient Tip: Choose sugar-free dark chocolate chips that use sugar substitutes like stevia or monk fruit. Look for brands such as Lily's (with stevia) or Lakanto (with monk fruit).

HARVEST FRUIT CRISP

DAIRY-FREE | GLUTEN-FREE | VEGAN | ONE-POT | QUICK

With an oat-based crisp and lots of whole fruit, this recipe packs in dietary fiber and potassium, suitable for cholesterol and blood pressure control.

Serves 6
Prep time: 10 minutes
Sauté: 2 minutes
Cook time: 3 minutes at high pressure
Pressure release: Natural for 10 minutes, then Quick
Total time: 30 minutes

FOR THE CRISP

6 small dates, pitted

2½ teaspoons avocado oil

½ cup gluten-free rolled oats

2 tablespoons sliced almonds

Nonstick cooking spray

FOR THE FILLING

3 medium apples, cored and sliced

3 medium pears, cored and sliced

2 tablespoons dried cranberries

1 tablespoon cornstarch

2 teaspoons brown sugar

Juice of 1 medium lemon

PER SERVING (ABOUT ½ CUP FRUIT AND 2 TABLESPOONS CRISP): Calories 198, Total Fat 4g, Saturated Fat 1g, Cholesterol 0mg, Sodium 3mg, Potassium 301mg, Magnesium 30mg, Carbohydrates 43g, Sugars 26g, Added Sugars 3g, Fiber 7g, Protein 2g, Vitamin K 8mcg

TO MAKE THE CRISP

1 In a food processor, combine the dates and oil. Process for a minute, then add the oats and pulse just a few times. Remove the blade and scrape down the bowl. Stir in the almonds.

2 Lightly coat the Instant Pot with nonstick spray. Select Sauté and wait 30 seconds for the Instant Pot to warm. Add the crisp mixture and heat for 2 minutes, stirring a few times, until lightly toasted. Press Cancel. Leave the mixture in the pot for 2 minutes more, then transfer to a small bowl.

TO MAKE THE FILLING

3 Pour the apples, pears, cranberries, cornstarch, brown sugar, and lemon juice into the Instant Pot and stir well.

4 Lock the lid into place. Select Pressure Cook and cook on high pressure for 3 minutes. When the cooking is complete, allow the pressure to release naturally for 10 minutes, then quick release any remaining pressure and remove the lid.

5 Divide the fruit mixture among six small bowls or ramekins. Top each with about 2 tablespoons of the crisp.

Variation Tip: For an extra-special treat, add a small scoop of low-fat vanilla frozen yogurt to each serving.

SAVORY MUFFINS WITH MIXED BERRY CHIA JAM

DAIRY-FREE | GLUTEN-FREE | VEGETARIAN | WORTH THE WAIT

White cannellini beans give these biscuits much of the starch they need for their overall texture while boosting their dietary fiber. With less added sugar than traditional jams, the chia jam still has enough sweetness, thanks to the berries and a bit of maple syrup.

Serves 4
Prep time: 5 minutes
Cook time: 20 minutes at high pressure
Pressure release: Natural for 12 minutes, then Quick
Total time: 1 hour 7 minutes (including time to make the jam)

1½ cups water

Nonstick cooking spray

1 cup low-sodium canned cannellini beans, drained and rinsed

2½ tablespoons olive oil, divided

1 medium egg

2 tablespoons unsweetened oat milk or low-fat milk

¼ cup all-purpose flour

½ teaspoon baking soda

½ teaspoon baking powder

¼ teaspoon salt

½ teaspoon dried rosemary, or 1½ teaspoons minced fresh rosemary

½ cup Mixed Berry Chia Jam (page 124)

1 Pour 1½ cups of water into the Instant Pot and set the trivet in the center. Lightly coat a 7-cup silicone egg mold with nonstick spray.

2 In a food processor, combine the beans and 2 tablespoons of oil, then process for 1 minute until creamy. Transfer to a medium bowl and mix in the egg, oat milk, and remaining ½ tablespoon of oil. Mix in the flour, baking soda, baking powder, salt, and rosemary.

3 Distribute the batter evenly among the wells of the prepared egg mold so each well is three-quarters full. Place the mold on top of the trivet.

4 Lock the lid into place. Select Pressure Cook and cook on high pressure for 20 minutes. When the cooking is complete, allow the pressure to release naturally for 12 minutes, then quick release any remaining pressure and remove the lid.

5 Top each muffin with 2 tablespoons of chia jam and serve.

PER SERVING (1 MUFFIN AND 2 TABLESPOONS CHIA JAM): Calories 132, Total Fat 7g, Saturated Fat 1g, Cholesterol 27mg, Sodium 159mg, Potassium 105mg, Magnesium 30mg, Carbohydrates 14g, Sugars 4g, Added Sugars 1g, Fiber 3g, Protein 4g, Vitamin K 22mcg

PEACH AND BLUEBERRY COBBLER

DAIRY-FREE | VEGAN | ONE-POT

The wild blueberries in this dreamy cobbler add a hefty dose of anthocyanin antioxidants, which are an anti-inflammatory for your heart and also great for brain health. While you could go with regular blueberries, these tiny deep-hued gems provide twice the antioxidants of the larger variety.

Serves 6
Prep time: 10 minutes
Sauté: 3 minutes
Cook time: 10 minutes at high pressure
Pressure release: Natural for 6 minutes, then Quick
Total time: 34 minutes

6 medium peaches, pitted and sliced

1 tablespoon cornstarch

3 tablespoons plus 2 teaspoons brown sugar (not packed), divided

2 teaspoons ground cinnamon, divided

½ cup water

¼ cup plus 2 tablespoons all-purpose flour

¼ teaspoon salt

½ teaspoon vanilla extract

1 cup frozen wild blueberries, thawed

PER SERVING (½ CUP): Calories 188, Total Fat 7g, Saturated Fat 1g, Cholesterol 0mg, Sodium 102mg, Potassium 318mg, Magnesium 18mg, Carbohydrates 30g, Sugars 20g, Added Sugars 5g, Fiber 3g, Protein 2g, Vitamin K 14mcg

1. Pour the peaches into the Instant Pot and add the cornstarch, 2 teaspoons of brown sugar, and 1 teaspoon of cinnamon. Stir well to combine. Add the water. Select Sauté and cook for about 3 minutes, until the water starts to boil. Press Cancel.

2. In a small bowl, combine the remaining 3 tablespoons of brown sugar, remaining 1 teaspoon of cinnamon, the flour, salt, and vanilla and mix until a gritty paste forms. Dollop the mixture onto the peaches in 6 spoonfuls.

3. Lock the lid into place. Select Pressure Cook and cook on high pressure for 10 minutes. When the cooking is complete, allow the pressure to release naturally for 6 minutes, then quick release any remaining pressure and remove the lid.

4. Press Cancel. Gently stir in the wild blueberries. Serve immediately.

BAKED APPLES WITH CRANBERRY-WALNUT FILLING

**DAIRY-FREE | GLUTEN-FREE | VEGAN | 5 OR FEWER INGREDIENTS
ONE-POT | QUICK**

Apples are filled with heart-healthy fiber, including the soluble fiber that's good for cholesterol control, while cinnamon supports healthy blood sugar levels. And with only a minimal amount of sodium (3 milligrams), these baked apples are perfect for those who need to control their blood pressure.

Serves 4
Prep time: 10 minutes
Cook time: 7 minutes at high pressure
Pressure release: Natural for 5 minutes, then Quick
Total time: 27 minutes

1½ cups water
4 medium Honeycrisp or Pink Lady apples
⅓ cup walnut pieces
2 tablespoons sweetened dried cranberries
1 tablespoon brown sugar
1 teaspoon ground cinnamon
1 tablespoon avocado oil

PER SERVING (1 STUFFED APPLE): Calories 194, Total Fat 8g, Saturated Fat 1g, Cholesterol 0mg, Sodium 3mg, Potassium 232mg, Magnesium 20mg, Carbohydrates 33g, Sugars 24g, Added Sugars 6g, Fiber 5g, Protein 2g, Vitamin K 8mcg

1. Pour 1½ cups of water into the Instant Pot and set the trivet in the center. Core the apples, leaving the bottom intact to form a cup.

2. In a food processor, combine the walnuts and cranberries. Pulse a few times until they form a crumbly consistency. Transfer the mixture to a small bowl. Add the brown sugar, cinnamon, and oil. Mix until well combined.

3. Stuff the apples with equal amounts of the walnut mixture; pack it in well. Place the stuffed apples on the trivet.

4. Lock the lid into place. Select Pressure Cook and cook on high pressure for 7 minutes. When the cooking is complete, allow the pressure to release naturally for 5 minutes, then quick release any remaining pressure and remove the lid.

5. Gently remove each stuffed apple with tongs and serve warm.

Variation Tip: If you don't have cranberries, an equal quantity of raisins will do. For a different flavor, use chopped dried apricots and pistachios in place of the walnuts.

CINNAMON-VANILLA CUSTARD

**DAIRY-FREE | GLUTEN-FREE | VEGETARIAN | 5 OR FEWER INGREDIENTS
WORTH THE WAIT**

*Because this custard doesn't contain much sugar, you'll enjoy its delightful
creaminess without a glycemic rush. It's sweetened with vanilla and cinnamon,
the latter of which is useful for blood sugar control.*

Serves 4
Prep time: 5 minutes
Cook time: 10 minutes at
high pressure
Pressure release: Quick
Total time: 1 hour
(including cooling time)

Nonstick cooking spray

3 medium eggs,
lightly whisked

1½ cups unsweetened
oat milk

1 teaspoon vanilla extract

1 teaspoon ground cinna-
mon, divided

2 tablespoons brown sugar
or granulated sugar

1½ cups water

PER SERVING: Calories 124,
Total Fat 6g, Saturated Fat 1g,
Cholesterol 123mg, Sodium
88mg, Potassium 95mg,
Magnesium 4mg, Carbohydrates
14g, Sugars 8g, Added Sugars
6g, Fiber 1g, Protein 5g,
Vitamin K 0mcg

1 Lightly coat a 6-inch round cake pan with nonstick spray.

2 In a medium bowl, combine the eggs, milk, vanilla,
½ teaspoon of cinnamon, and the sugar. Whisk
until well combined. Pour into the prepared cake
pan and loosely cover with aluminum foil.

3 Pour 1½ cups of water into the Instant Pot and
set the trivet in the center. Place the cake pan on
the trivet.

4 Lock the lid into place. Select Pressure Cook
and cook on high pressure for 7 minutes. Quick
release the pressure. Remove the foil and give the
custard a good whisk. Return the foil, place the
pan back in the Instant Pot, lock the lid, and cook
for another 3 minutes on high pressure. When
the cooking is complete, quick release the pressure and remove the lid.

5 Remove the cake pan and the foil and let cool for
15 minutes.

6 Dust with the remaining ½ teaspoon of cinnamon. For best results, refrigerate for another
20 minutes until cool before serving.

Flavor Boost: For a sweeter touch, drizzle on 2 teaspoons
of maple syrup before serving (this adds 8 grams of
added sugars, still within heart-healthy guidelines).

CHIA-PEACH "MOCHI" CAKE

DAIRY-FREE | GLUTEN-FREE | VEGETARIAN | WORTH THE WAIT

Mochi is a Japanese dessert made with sticky rice that has a soft, stretchy, chewy texture. (You may have heard of mochi ice cream, in which the mochi batter surrounds a little ball of ice cream.) Using chia in this mochi-inspired cake brings anti-inflammatory omega-3s to the mix and also creates a lighter consistency. It also means you won't need eggs, making this a no-cholesterol treat.

Serves 6
Prep time: 15 minutes
Cook time: 20 minutes at high pressure
Pressure release: Natural for 5 minutes, then Quick
Total time: 1 hour (including cooling time)

1½ cups water
Nonstick cooking spray
1 tablespoon chia seeds
¼ cup water
¼ cup honey
½ cup unsweetened oat milk
1½ tablespoons avocado oil
½ cup brown rice flour
3 tablespoons unsweetened shredded coconut
1 medium peach, pitted and chopped

1 Pour 1½ cups of water into the Instant Pot and set the trivet in the center. Lightly coat a 6-inch springform cake pan with nonstick spray. Fold an 18-inch sheet of foil lengthwise into thirds so it forms a 4-inch-wide strip. Place the foil strip over the trivet so the ends overhang the trivet evenly (this will make it easier to remove the pan from the Instant Pot after cooking).

2 In a medium bowl, combine the chia seeds and water. Allow it to gel for 10 minutes, then add the honey, milk, oil, and flour and mix until well combined. Fold in the coconut and peaches. Pour the batter into the prepared pan. Set the pan over the foil strip on the trivet, then fold the ends of the strip over the pan so you can close the lid.

3 Lock the lid into place. Select Pressure Cook and cook on high pressure for 20 minutes. When the cooking is complete, allow the pressure to release naturally for 5 minutes, then quick release any remaining pressure and remove the lid.

PER SERVING (1 SLICE): Calories 113, Total Fat 6g, Saturated Fat 2g, Cholesterol 0mg, Sodium 11mg, Potassium 91mg, Magnesium 24mg, Carbohydrates 13g, Sugars 1g, Added Sugars 1g, Fiber 2g, Protein 2g, Vitamin K 15mcg

4   Remove the pan from the Instant Pot and let cool for 15 minutes before serving. Unlatch and gently remove the springform ring, then slice the cake into 6 wedges and serve. (Note: If you are using a regular 6-inch round cake pan, run your knife between the edge of the pan and the cake, then cut the cake into 6 wedges. Guide the first slice out with a small butter knife, and the rest should come out easily.)

Variation Tip: You can use a white peach instead of the traditional yellow peach if you prefer a sweeter flavor.

CHEESECAKE WITH MIXED BERRY CHIA JAM

To keep the saturated fat low, Neufchâtel cheese replaces regular cream cheese (it's got one-third less fat) and is paired with low-fat cottage cheese to achieve the classic creamy density of a cheesecake without the excess fat.

Serves 6
Prep time: 10 minutes
Cook time: 25 minutes at high pressure
Pressure release: Natural for 10 minutes, then Quick
Total time: 1 hour 40 minutes (including time to make the jam, plus cooling time)

1½ cups water

Nonstick cooking spray

2 medium eggs, lightly beaten

4 ounces Neufchâtel cheese or low-fat cream cheese

6 ounces low-fat cottage cheese

½ teaspoon vanilla extract

2 tablespoons confectioners' sugar

1 tablespoon cornstarch

½ batch Mixed Berry Chia Jam (page 124)

PER SERVING (1 SLICE): Calories 129, Total Fat 7g, Saturated Fat 3g, Cholesterol 72mg, Sodium 173mg, Potassium 95mg, Magnesium 10mg, Carbohydrates 10g, Sugars 3g, Added Sugars 3g, Fiber 1g, Protein 7g, Vitamin K 12mcg

1. Pour 1½ cups of water into the Instant Pot and set the trivet in the center. Lightly coat a 6-inch springform cake pan with nonstick spray. Fold an 18-inch sheet of foil lengthwise into thirds so it forms a 4-inch-wide strip. Place the foil strip over the trivet so the ends overhang the trivet evenly (this will make it easier to remove the pan from the Instant Pot after cooking).

2. In a food processor, combine the eggs, Neufchâtel, cottage cheese, vanilla, confectioners' sugar, and cornstarch. Process for about 1 minute, until smooth and creamy. Transfer to the prepared cake pan and set the pan over the foil strip on the trivet, then fold the ends of the strip over the pan so you can close the lid.

3. Lock the lid into place. Select Pressure Cook and cook on high pressure for 25 minutes. When the cooking is complete, allow the pressure to release naturally for 10 minutes, then quick release any remaining pressure and remove the lid.

4. Carefully remove the pan from the Instant Pot and let cool for 15 minutes, then refrigerate for another 10 minutes before serving.

5. Spread the chia jam over the top of the cheesecake, slice into 6 wedges, and serve.

MIXED BERRY CHIA JAM, PAGE 124

CHAPTER 8
SAUCES AND STAPLES

SWEET-AND-TANGY BBQ SAUCE

DAIRY-FREE | GLUTEN-FREE | VEGETARIAN | 5 OR FEWER INGREDIENTS
ONE-POT | QUICK

The fire-roasted tomatoes keep this sauce rich and flavorful, and low-sodium, low-sugar ketchup makes it heart-healthier than your typical salty, sugary barbecue sauce. When choosing a ketchup, look for one that contains 50 percent less sodium and sugar (75 milligrams of sodium and 2 grams of added sugars per tablespoon) than traditional ketchup.

Makes 1 cup
Prep time: 5 minutes
Sauté: 3 minutes
Total time: 8 minutes

1 cup canned fire-roasted crushed or diced tomatoes

6 tablespoons low-sodium, low-sugar ketchup

2 teaspoons garlic powder

½ teaspoon low-sodium Worcestershire sauce

PER SERVING (2 TABLESPOONS):
Calories 23, Total Fat 0g, Saturated Fat 0g, Cholesterol 0mg, Sodium 133mg, Potassium 115mg, Magnesium 1mg, Carbohydrates 5g, Sugars 2g, Added Sugars 1.5g, Fiber 1g, Protein 0g, Vitamin K 0mcg

1 Pour the tomatoes, ketchup, garlic powder, and Worcestershire sauce into the Instant Pot and stir to combine. Select Sauté and cook for 3 minutes, or until it starts to boil. Press Cancel.

2 Serve what you plan to use immediately and store the remainder in an airtight container in the fridge for up to 1 week.

Substitution Tip: If you don't have low-sodium, low-sugar ketchup, you can use an equal amount of tomato paste plus ¼ teaspoon of low-sodium soy sauce.

SWEET-AND-SOUR ORANGE SAUCE

DAIRY-FREE | GLUTEN-FREE | VEGETARIAN | QUICK

This sauce has only 4 grams of added sugars and is low in sodium (just 50 grams per serving), keeping it heart-healthy indeed. The Orange Chicken with Kale and Carrot Salad (page 78) uses this sweet-and-sour sauce, and it is a perfect dipping sauce for Spring Rolls with Seasoned Ground Pork (page 46).

Makes 1¾ cups
Prep time: 5 minutes
Sauté: 4 minutes
Cook time: 2 minutes at high pressure
Pressure release: Natural for 5 minutes, then Quick
Total time: 21 minutes

2 teaspoons cornstarch

2 teaspoons water

1 cup canned pineapple chunks

1 large red bell pepper, chopped

Juice of 1 medium orange

1½ tablespoons honey

¼ cup unseasoned rice vinegar

⅛ teaspoon salt

PER SERVING (⅓ CUP): Calories 52, Total Fat 0g, Saturated Fat 0g, Cholesterol 0mg, Sodium 51mg, Potassium 119mg, Magnesium 8mg, Carbohydrates 13g, Sugars 9g, Added Sugars 4g, Fiber 1g, Protein 1g, Vitamin K 2mcg

1 In a small cup, mix together the cornstarch and water. Set aside.

2 Combine the pineapple, bell pepper, orange juice, honey, and vinegar in the Instant Pot. Stir well. Select Sauté and cook for 3 to 4 minutes, until the mixture starts to simmer, then stir in the cornstarch mixture.

3 Lock the lid into place. Select Pressure Cook and cook on high pressure for 2 minutes. When the cooking is complete, allow the pressure to release naturally for 5 minutes, then quick release any remaining pressure and remove the lid.

4 Transfer the mixture to a food processor or blender, add the salt, and process for 30 seconds to 1 minute, until pureed. Let cool, then transfer to an airtight container and store in the refrigerator for up to 1 week.

Flavor Boost: For an aromatic addition, add in a pinch of Chinese five-spice powder before pureeing.

LOW-SODIUM TERIYAKI SAUCE

DAIRY-FREE | VEGETARIAN | QUICK

Teriyaki sauces are often high in sugar and sodium. This version uses just enough honey to enhance the natural sweetness of the pineapple. Low-sodium soy sauce keeps it just under 240 milligrams of sodium per serving. Teriyaki sauce is wonderful on chicken, pork, and salmon. It is a great way to add more pizzazz to leftovers like rice or even sweet potatoes.

Makes ½ cup
Prep time: 5 minutes
Sauté: 5 minutes
Total time: 10 minutes

½ cup canned crushed
   pineapple

1 tablespoon honey

1 tablespoon unseasoned
   rice vinegar

2½ tablespoons
   low-sodium soy sauce

1 garlic clove, crushed

1 teaspoon grated
   fresh ginger

PER SERVING (4 TEASPOONS):
Calories 28, Total Fat 0g,
Saturated Fat 0g, Cholesterol
0mg, Sodium 239mg, Potassium
57mg, Magnesium 5mg,
Carbohydrates 7g, Sugars 6g,
Added Sugars 3g, Fiber 0g,
Protein 1g, Vitamin K 0mcg

1 Combine the pineapple, honey, vinegar, soy sauce, garlic, and ginger in the Instant Pot. Stir well. Select Sauté and cook for 3 minutes, or until it starts to boil. Stir and cook for 2 minutes more, until the liquid starts to cook down and thicken. Press Cancel.

2 Transfer the mixture to a food processor or blender and process for about 1 minute, until smooth. Let cool, then transfer to an airtight container and store in the refrigerator for up to 1 week.

Flavor Boost: Add some freshly ground black pepper to enhance the tangy-sweet punch.

ZESTY CARROT TOMATO SAUCE

DAIRY-FREE | VEGAN | ONE-POT

Low in sugar and sodium, this zesty marinara is a great staple to have on hand. Naturally sweet carrots and red bell pepper help balance out the acidity of the tomatoes. Whether you are making pizza or pasta or simply want to enhance a chicken dish, this sauce offers that comforting appeal.

Makes 4 cups
Prep time: 5 minutes
Sauté: 9 minutes
Cook time: 6 minutes at high pressure
Pressure release: Natural for 6 minutes, then Quick
Total time: 31 minutes

2 teaspoons olive oil

½ medium yellow onion, chopped

1 large red or orange bell pepper, sliced

2 garlic cloves, minced

2 medium carrots, chopped

1 (14.5-ounce) can low-sodium crushed tomatoes

1 (14-ounce) can diced fire-roasted tomatoes

2 teaspoons low-sodium soy sauce

1 tablespoon Italian seasoning

PER SERVING (½ CUP): Calories 48, Total Fat 1g, Saturated Fat 0g, Cholesterol 0mg, Sodium 186mg, Potassium 310mg, Magnesium 13mg, Carbohydrates 8g, Sugars 4g, Added Sugars 1g, Fiber 3g, Protein 1g, Vitamin K 9mcg

1 Select Sauté and wait 30 seconds for the Instant Pot to warm. Pour in the oil and heat for 30 seconds until it starts to sizzle.

2 Add the onion and sauté for 5 minutes, stirring occasionally, until the onion softens. Add the bell pepper and continue to heat, stirring, for another 3 minutes.

3 Mix in the garlic, carrots, crushed tomatoes, fire-roasted tomatoes, soy sauce, and Italian seasoning.

4 Lock the lid into place. Select Pressure Cook and cook on high pressure for 6 minutes. When the cooking is complete, allow the pressure to release naturally for 6 minutes, then quick release any remaining pressure and unlock the lid.

5 Serve warm. If you have any leftovers or are preparing a batch in advance, transfer the sauce to three 16-ounce glass jars or a large (6-cup) glass container and cool before sealing with airtight lid(s). Refrigerate for up to 5 days.

RATATOUILLE BASE

DAIRY-FREE | VEGETARIAN | ONE-POT

This ratatouille is delicious on its own, as a side, or as a spread (like a bruschetta topping). With an array of veggies, you'll get a hefty dose of blood pressure–regulating potassium and dietary fiber.

Makes 6 cups
Prep time: 10 minutes
Sauté: 13 minutes
Cook time: 6 minutes at high pressure
Pressure release: Natural for 6 minutes, then Quick
Total time: 40 minutes

1 tablespoon olive oil

1 medium yellow onion, chopped

2 medium zucchini, or 1 medium yellow squash and 1 medium zucchini

3 garlic cloves, minced

1 medium eggplant, cubed

3 medium heirloom or Roma (plum) tomatoes, chopped

¼ cup tomato paste

1 cup canned pumpkin puree

1 teaspoon honey

1 tablespoon low-sodium soy sauce

1 tablespoon Italian seasoning

PER SERVING (1 CUP): Calories 121, Total Fat 3g, Saturated Fat 1g, Cholesterol 0mg, Sodium 120mg, Potassium 966mg, Magnesium 62mg, Carbohydrates 22g, Sugars 13g, Added Sugars 1g, Fiber 7g, Protein 5g, Vitamin K 32mcg

1 Select Sauté and wait 30 seconds for the Instant Pot to warm. Pour in the oil and heat for 30 seconds until it starts to sizzle.

2 Add the onions and zucchini and sauté for 10 minutes, stirring occasionally, until the onions soften. Add 1 to 2 tablespoons water if needed to prevent them from sticking to the bottom of the pot.

3 Mix in the garlic, eggplant, tomatoes, tomato paste, pumpkin puree, honey, soy sauce, and Italian seasoning and sauté for 2 minutes more, until fragrant.

4 Lock the lid into place. Select Pressure Cook and cook on high pressure for 6 minutes. When the cooking is complete, allow the pressure to release naturally for 6 minutes, then quick release any remaining pressure and remove the lid.

5 Serve warm. If you have any leftovers or are preparing a batch in advance, transfer the ratatouille base to three 16-ounce glass jars or a large (6-cup) glass container and cool before sealing with airtight lid(s). Refrigerate for up to 5 days.

EASY CORN BREAD MUFFINS

DAIRY-FREE | VEGETARIAN | WORTH THE WAIT

These tasty corn muffins aren't over the top with added sugars. And because they are made with a minimal amount of oil and no butter, they are lower in saturated fat than traditional bakery muffins.

Makes 6 muffins
Prep time: 15 minutes
Cook time: 10 minutes at high pressure
Pressure release: Natural for 5 minutes, then Quick
Total time: 50 minutes (including cooling time)

¼ cup cornmeal
½ cup unsweetened soy milk
1 medium egg
1 tablespoon honey
1 tablespoon avocado oil
⅛ teaspoon salt
½ cup all-purpose flour
½ teaspoon baking soda
¼ cup frozen corn kernels
1½ cups water

PER SERVING (1 MUFFIN): Calories 71, Total Fat 4g, Saturated Fat 1g, Cholesterol 27mg, Sodium 170mg, Potassium 52mg, Magnesium 6mg, Carbohydrates 8g, Sugars 2g, Added Sugars 1g, Fiber 1g, Protein 2g, Vitamin K 3mcg

1 Lightly coat a 7-cup silicone egg mold with non-stick spray.

2 In a medium bowl, soak the cornmeal in the soy milk for 10 minutes. Stir in the egg, honey, and oil until well combined. Then add the salt, flour, baking soda, and corn.

3 Divide the batter evenly among six wells of the egg mold. Cover the mold with its lid or aluminum foil.

4 Pour 1½ cups of water into the Instant Pot and set the trivet in the center. Place the egg mold on the trivet.

5 Lock the lid into place. Select Pressure Cook and cook on high pressure for 10 minutes. When the cooking is complete, allow the pressure to release naturally for 5 minutes, then quick release any remaining pressure and remove the lid.

6 Carefully remove the egg mold from the Instant Pot and pop out the muffins onto a wire rack. Let cool for 15 minutes.

7 The muffins are best eaten fresh, but you can store them in an airtight container at room temperature for 1 day.

STEAMED BUNS

DAIRY-FREE | VEGAN | WORTH THE WAIT

Steamed buns can be filled with savory or sweet ingredients, making them a versatile snack, appetizer, or even dessert. These buns are low in saturated fat and contain very little added sugar. They are a great base for adding a little protein, healthy fat, and/or fiber—try the baked apple filling made with cranberries and walnuts on page 108.

Makes 15 buns
Prep time: 10 minutes, plus 2 hours rising time
Sauté: 35 minutes
Total time: 2 hours 45 minutes

1 (¼-ounce) packet active dry yeast
1 tablespoon plus 1 teaspoon sugar, divided
1¾ cups all-purpose flour, divided
¾ cup warm water, divided
1 tablespoon sugar, divided
⅛ teaspoon salt
½ teaspoon baking powder
1 tablespoon olive oil
1½ cups water
Nonstick cooking spray

1 In a medium bowl, combine the yeast, 1 teaspoon of sugar, ¼ cup of flour, and ¼ cup of warm water. Let the mixture sit for 30 minutes until it's foamy.

2 Once it's foamy, add the remaining 1 tablespoon of sugar, remaining 1½ cups of flour, remaining ½ cup of warm water, the salt, baking powder, and oil and stir until the dough comes together. Knead the dough for about 2 minutes, until it is smooth and stretchy. If you need a little flour on your hands to reduce stickiness, use 1 tablespoon at a time as needed.

3 Coat a large bowl with nonstick spray. Transfer the dough to the bowl, cover, and let rest at room temperature for 1 hour, until it doubles in size.

4 Separate the dough in half and then form 15 balls. Place the dough balls on a floured cutting board, cover with a clean kitchen towel, and let sit for 30 minutes.

PER SERVING (1 BUN): Calories 72, Total Fat 1g, Saturated Fat 0.2g, Cholesterol 0mg, Sodium 63mg, Potassium 22mg, Magnesium 4mg, Carbohydrates 13g, Sugars 1g, Added Sugars 1g, Fiber 1g, Protein 2g, Vitamin K 1mcg

5   Pour 1½ cups of water into the Instant Pot and set the trivet in the center. Select Sauté and bring the water to a boil, about 6 minutes.

6   Turn a 6-inch round cake pan upside-down and coat with nonstick spray. Evenly space 4 buns on the bottom of the pan. Carefully place the pan on top of the trivet. Cover the inner liner with a clean kitchen towel and steam for 7 to 8 minutes, until the buns are fluffy. Transfer the buns to a wire rack to cool. Repeat the process three times with the remaining dough (coat the pan with more nonstick spray as needed).

7   The buns are best eaten fresh, but you can store them at room temperature in an airtight container for one day.

Flavor Boost: Add 1 teaspoon of garlic powder along with the salt and baking powder in step 2 to make the buns more savory.

MIXED BERRY CHIA JAM

While many chia jams have you add chia directly to the stewed fruit, I like to gel mine first with a 1:3 ratio of chia to water. This allows the chia to soak up a bit more liquid and expand to a great jammy consistency. Chia seeds provide omega-3s and fiber, giving them twofold benefits for heart health—they are anti-inflammatory and easy on the digestive system.

Makes 1 cup
Prep time: 10 minutes
Sauté: 5 minutes
Total time: 25 minutes
(including cooling time)

2 tablespoons chia seeds

6 tablespoons water

1½ cups frozen
   mixed berries

2 tablespoons fresh
   lemon juice

2 tablespoons maple syrup

PER SERVING (1 TABLESPOON):
Calories 15, Total Fat 0.5g,
Saturated Fat 0g, Cholesterol
0mg, Sodium 2mg, Potassium
9mg, Magnesium 5mg,
Carbohydrates 3g, Sugars 1g,
Added Sugars 1g, Fiber 1g,
Protein 0g, Vitamin K 9mcg

1 In a small bowl, soak the chia seeds in the water for 5 to 10 minutes until the chia gels.

2 Pour the berries, lemon juice, and maple syrup into the Instant Pot and select Sauté. Stir well and cook until the mixture comes to a boil, 3 to 4 minutes. Add the gelled chia seeds and stir for another minute. Press Cancel.

3 Transfer the jam to a jar and let cool, uncovered, for 15 minutes. If not using right away, seal the jar tightly and refrigerate for up to 5 days.

Variation Tip: The juice of a lime or mandarin orange can be used instead of lemon juice for a similar tang. I sometimes run out of lemons, but often have mandarins around because they are such an easy, portable snack.

CREAM OF MUSHROOM SOUP

VEGETARIAN | ONE-POT

Cream of mushroom soup is often high in sodium, but you can make this lower-sodium version in little time for a heart-smart option. Once it's done cooking, you'll use an immersion blender to process it until it's smooth and creamy. But if you leave some chunks of mushrooms, it adds a nice appealing texture.

Makes 2 cups
Prep time: 5 minutes
Sauté: 7 minutes
Cook time: 2 minutes at high pressure
Pressure release: Natural for 12 minutes, then Quick
Total time: 31 minutes

1 teaspoon olive oil
10 ounces sliced white button mushrooms
1 garlic clove, crushed
1 tablespoon champagne vinegar or white vinegar
2 tablespoons all-purpose flour
1 cup low-fat milk
½ cup water
1 bay leaf
½ teaspoon Italian seasoning
⅛ teaspoon salt

PER SERVING (½ CUP): Calories 88, Total Fat 4g, Saturated Fat 1g, Cholesterol 3mg, Sodium 105mg, Potassium 326mg, Magnesium 15mg, Carbohydrates 9g, Sugars 5g, Added Sugars 0g, Fiber 1g, Protein 5g, Vitamin K 4mcg

1 Select Sauté and wait 30 seconds for the Instant Pot to warm. Pour in the oil and heat for 30 seconds until it starts to sizzle.

2 Add the mushrooms and sauté for 5 minutes, until they start to cook down. Then add the garlic and stir for 30 seconds, until fragrant. Add the vinegar and scrape any crisp bits from the bottom of the pan with a spatula.

3 Whisk in the flour and milk until well incorporated. Then add the water, bay leaf, and Italian seasoning.

4 Lock the lid into place. Select Pressure Cook and cook on high pressure for 2 minutes. When the cooking is complete, allow the pressure to release naturally for 12 minutes, then quick release any remaining pressure and remove the lid.

5 Remove the bay leaf, add the salt, and use an immersion blender to get a smooth consistency. If desired, leave a few chunks of mushrooms for texture.

SIMPLE VEGGIE BROTH

DAIRY-FREE | VEGAN | QUICK

With just under 200 milligrams of sodium per 1-cup serving, this flavorful vegetable broth beats commercial brands in both taste and reduced sodium content. Cooking veggies under pressure builds flavor, which is often lackluster in most commercial low-sodium vegetable broths.

Makes 4 cups
Prep time: 5 minutes
Sauté: 6 minutes
Cook time: 2 minutes at high pressure
Pressure release: Natural for 5 minutes, then Quick
Total time: 23 minutes

2 teaspoons olive oil

½ medium red onion, chopped

4 cups water

1 cup chopped carrots

2 medium celery stalks, chopped

1 teaspoon garlic powder

1 tablespoon Italian seasoning

1 tablespoon low-sodium soy sauce

1 bay leaf

PER SERVING (1 CUP): Calories 52, Total Fat 0g, Saturated Fat 0g, Cholesterol 0mg, Sodium 197mg, Potassium 233mg, Magnesium 18mg, Carbohydrates 7g, Sugars 3g, Added Sugars 0g, Fiber 2g, Protein 1g, Vitamin K 20mcg

1 Select Sauté and wait 30 seconds for the Instant Pot to warm. Pour in the oil and heat for 30 seconds until it starts to sizzle.

2 Add the onion and cook, stirring occasionally, for 5 minutes, until the onion softens. If the "hot" warning appears, add 1 to 2 tablespoons water.

3 Add the water, carrots, celery, garlic powder, Italian seasoning, soy sauce, and bay leaf.

4 Lock the lid into place. Select Pressure Cook and cook on high pressure for 2 minutes. When the cooking is complete, allow the pressure to release naturally for 5 minutes, then quick release any remaining pressure and remove the lid.

5 Strain the broth, discard the solids, and use right away, or let cool and then transfer to an airtight container. Refrigerate for up to 4 days or freeze for up to 3 months.

Substitution Tip: If you don't have celery, you can swap it out for 1 cup of chopped romaine lettuce.

MEASUREMENT CONVERSIONS

VOLUME EQUIVALENTS (LIQUID)

US Standard	US Standard (ounces)	Metric (approx.)
2 tablespoons	1 fl. oz.	30 mL
¼ cup	2 fl. oz.	60 mL
½ cup	4 fl. oz.	120 mL
1 cup	8 fl. oz.	240 mL
1½ cups	12 fl. oz.	355 mL
2 cups or 1 pint	16 fl. oz.	475 mL
4 cups or 1 quart	32 fl. oz.	1 L
1 gallon	128 fl. oz.	4 L

VOLUME EQUIVALENTS (DRY)

US Standard	Metric (approx.)
⅛ teaspoon	0.5 mL
¼ teaspoon	1 mL
½ teaspoon	2 mL
¾ teaspoon	4 mL
1 teaspoon	5 mL
1 tablespoon	15 mL
¼ cup	59 mL
⅓ cup	79 mL
½ cup	118 mL
⅔ cup	156 mL
¾ cup	177 mL
1 cup	235 mL
2 cups or 1 pint	475 mL
3 cups	700 mL
4 cups or 1 quart	1 L

OVEN TEMPERATURES

Fahrenheit (F)	Celsius (C) (approx.)
250°	120°
300°	150°
325°	165°
350°	180°
375°	190°
400°	200°
425°	220°
450°	230°

WEIGHT EQUIVALENTS

US Standard	Metric (approx.)
½ ounce	15 g
1 ounce	30 g
2 ounces	60 g
4 ounces	115 g
8 ounces	225 g
12 ounces	340 g
16 ounces or 1 pound	455 g

REFERENCES

"Antioxidants, Vitamin E, Beta Carotene, & Cardiovascular Disease." Cleveland Clinic. Accessed August 20, 2021. my.ClevelandClinic.org/health/articles /16740-antioxidants-vitamin-e-beta-carotene--cardiovascular-disease.

Carpenter, William E., Derek Lam, Glenn M. Toney, Neal L. Weintraub, and Zhenyu Qin. "Zinc, Copper, and Blood Pressure: Human Population Studies." *Medical Science Monitor* 19 (2013): 1–8. doi.org/10.12659/msm.883708.

"Cholesterol: Top foods to improve your numbers." Mayo Clinic. Mayo Foundation for Medical Education and Research, July 17, 2018. MayoClinic.org /diseases-conditions/high-blood-cholesterol/in-depth/cholesterol /art-20045192.

"Eating Fish Twice a Week Reduces Heart Stroke Risk." Heart.org. Accessed August 5, 2021. Heart.org/en/news/2018/05/25/eating-fish-twice-a -week-reduces-heart-stroke-risk.

Evert, Alison B., Michelle Dennison, Christopher D. Gardner, W. Timothy Garvey, Ka Hei Karen Lau, Janice MacLeod, Joanna Mitri, et al. "Nutrition Therapy for Adults with Diabetes or Prediabetes: A Consensus Report." Diabetes Care. American Diabetes Association, May 1, 2019. care.DiabetesJournals.org /content/42/5/731.

"Heart-Check Recipe Certification Program Nutrition Requirements." Heart.org. Accessed August 20, 2021. Heart.org/en/healthy-living/company -collaboration/heart-check-certification/heart-check-certified -recipes/heart-check-recipe-certification-program-nutrition -requirements.

Houston, Mark. "The Role of Magnesium in Hypertension and Cardiovascular Disease." *The Journal of Clinical Hypertension* 13, no. 11 (2011): 843–47. doi.org/10.1111/j.1751-7176.2011.00538.x.

Illinois, University of. "Warfarin and Diet." Healthline. Healthline Media, July 8, 2019. Healthline.com/health/dvt/warfarin-diet#foods-to-limit.

"Key Minerals to Help Control Blood Pressure." Harvard Health, May 3, 2019. health.Harvard.edu/heart-health/key-minerals-to-help-control -blood-pressure.

Kolahi, Sousan, Bahram Pourghassem Gargari, Mehran Mesgari Abbasi, Mohammad Asghari Jafarabadi, and Neda Ghamarzad Shishavan. "Effects of Phylloquinone Supplementation on Lipid Profile in Women with Rheumatoid Arthritis: A Double Blind Placebo Controlled Study." *Nutrition Research and Practice* 9, no. 2 (2015): 186. doi.org/10.4162/nrp.2015.9.2.186.

Krittanawong, Chayakrit, Ameesh Isath, Joshua Hahn, Zhen Wang, Sonya E. Fogg, Dhrubajyoti Bandyopadhyay, Hani Jneid, Salim S. Virani, and W.H. Wilson Tang. "Mushroom Consumption and Cardiovascular Health: A Systematic Review." *The American Journal of Medicine* 134, no. 5 (2021). doi.org/10.1016/j.amjmed.2020.10.035.

Legarth, Christian, Daniela Grimm, Markus Wehland, Johann Bauer, and Marcus Krüger. "The Impact of Vitamin D in the Treatment of Essential Hypertension." *International Journal of Molecular Sciences* 19, no. 2 (2018): 455. doi.org/10.3390/ijms19020455.

Leiser, S. "Peer Review #2 of 'Chlorophyll Enhances Oxidative Stress Tolerance in Caenorhabditis Elegans and Extends Its Lifespan (v0.1)'," 2016. doi.org/10.7287/peerj.1879v0.1/reviews/2.

Mehta, Varshil, and Shivika Agarwal. "Does Vitamin D Deficiency Lead to Hypertension?" *Cureus*, 2017. doi.org/10.7759/cureus.1038.

"Omega-3 in Fish: How Eating Fish Helps Your Heart." Mayo Clinic. Mayo Foundation for Medical Education and Research, September 28, 2019. MayoClinic .org/diseases-conditions/heart-disease/in-depth/omega-3/art-20045614.

Orrange, Sharon. "These Drugs Can Mess with Your Potassium Levels." The GoodRx Prescription Savings Blog, March 23, 2019. GoodRx.com /blog/these-drugs-can-mess-with-your-potassium.

"Reducing Sodium in Canned Beans - Easier than 1-2-3." Today's Dietitian. Accessed August 5, 2021. TodaysDietitian.com/newarchives/011110p62 .shtml.

"Rinse Beans the Right Way to Reduce Sodium." Bean Institute. Accessed August 5, 2021. BeanInstitute.com/rinse-beans-the-right-way -to-reduce-sodium.

Sheldon G. Sheps, M.D. "Warfarin Diet: What Foods Should I Avoid?" Mayo Clinic. Mayo Foundation for Medical Education and Research, February 16, 2021. MayoClinic.org/diseases-conditions/thrombophlebitis/expert -answers/warfarin/faq-20058443.

Swain, Janis F., Phyllis B. McCarron, Eileen F. Hamilton, Frank M. Sacks, and Lawrence J. Appel. "Characteristics of the Diet Patterns Tested in the Optimal Macronutrient Intake Trial to Prevent Heart Disease (OmniHeart): Options for a Heart-Healthy Diet." *Journal of the American Dietetic Association* 108, no. 2 (2008): 257–65. doi.org/10.1016/j.jada.2007.10.040.

INDEX

ACKNOWLEDGMENTS

I'd like to thank my husband, JP, and daughters, Ailish and Julia, for once again allowing me the space to develop a collection of recipes for the umpteenth time. I also have to thank my dear friend Bridie for her moral support and feedback and especially for loaning me her Instant Pot and silicone egg mold to help expedite the development of my recipes for this book. And finally, I'd like to thank my editor, Justin Hartung, for elevating my writing to the next level.

ABOUT THE AUTHOR

Lauren O'Connor, MS, RDN, is a registered dietitian, a yoga instructor, and the author of several cookbooks, including *Healthy Cooking for One.* She offers nutritional counseling and consulting services for individuals and companies nationwide. A member of the Academy of Nutrition and Dietetics (AND) and Food & Culinary Professionals (FCP), she received her master's degree in nutritional sciences from California State University, Los Angeles, and has completed an advanced culinary nutrition certification through Culinary Nutrition Studio, LLC. As a recipe developer, writer, and credentialed health advocate, she contributes to various print, television, and online media.

O'Connor promotes whole-food choices in her plant-based nutritional guidelines, tailoring plans and recipes to best suit her clients' needs. With knowledge of gastroesophageal reflux disease (GERD) healing and management, she promotes dietary and lifestyle practices to improve health outcomes for those with acid reflux concerns. You can learn more on her website, NutriSavvyHealth.com.